Keith Pepperell

Photographs II

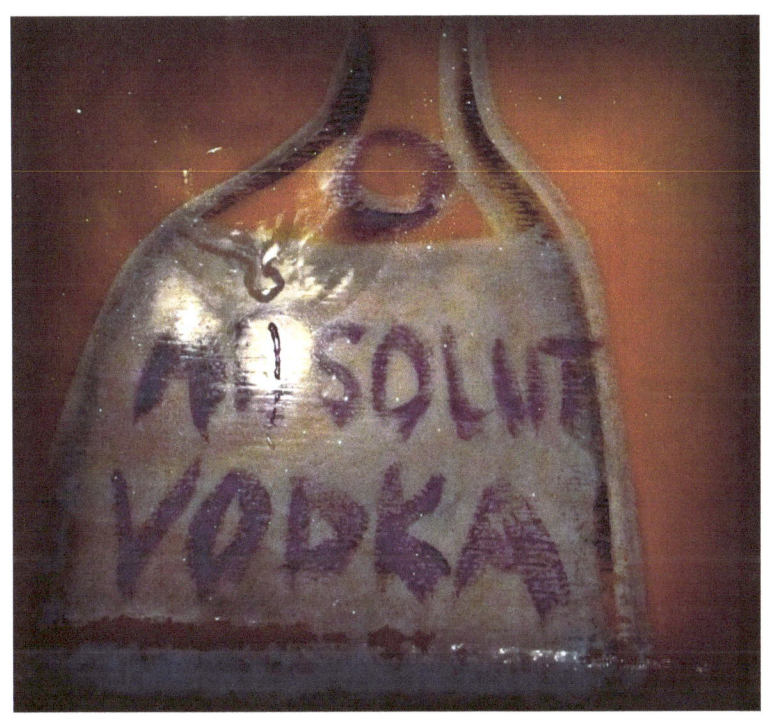

Keith Pepperell

ISBN-13: 978-1543066081

ISBN-10: 1543066089

DEDICATION

To my spawn Jack, Lydia, and Alex all of whom have taken
a snap of something at one time or another

ACKNOWLEDGMENTS

Don Fowler

Audrey Fowler

Pep Pepperell

Joan Pepperell

All of whom were dab hands with a camera

THE PICTURES

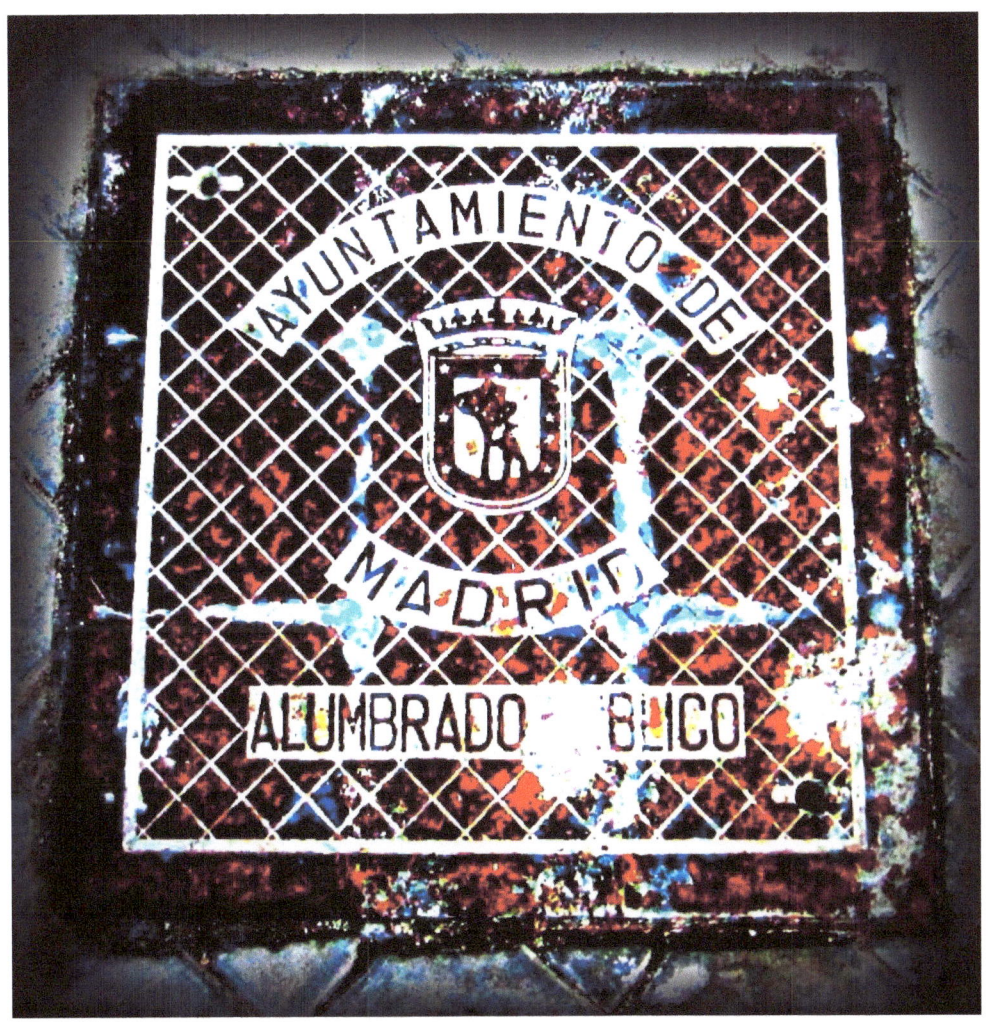

Madrid

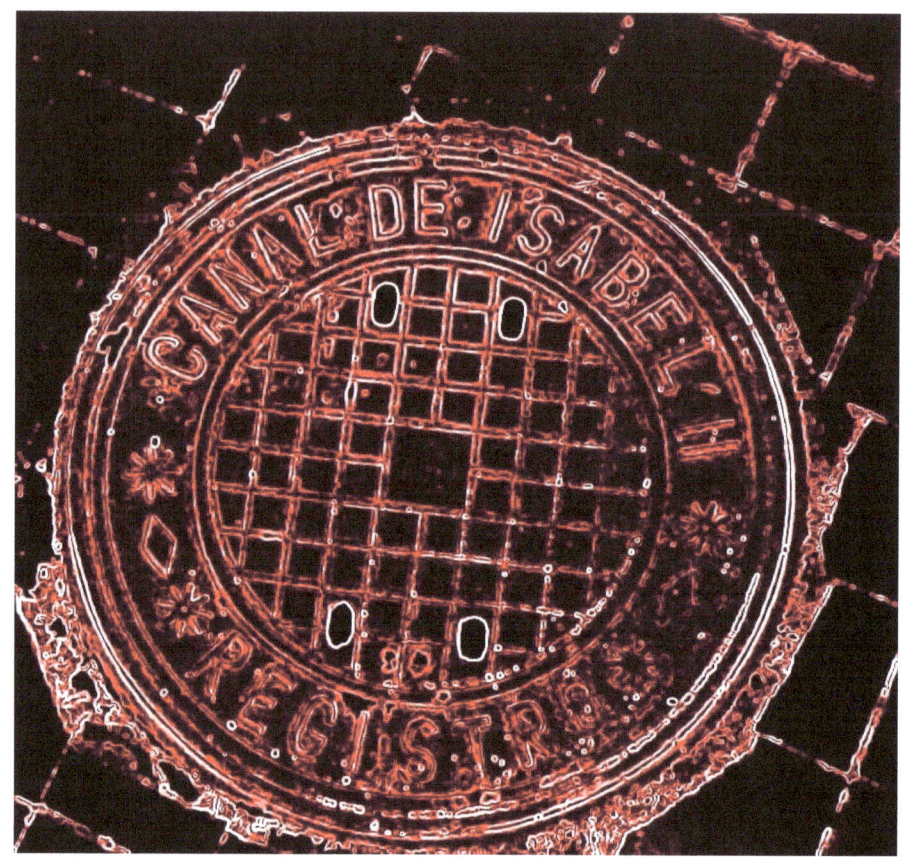

Manhole Cover, Madrid

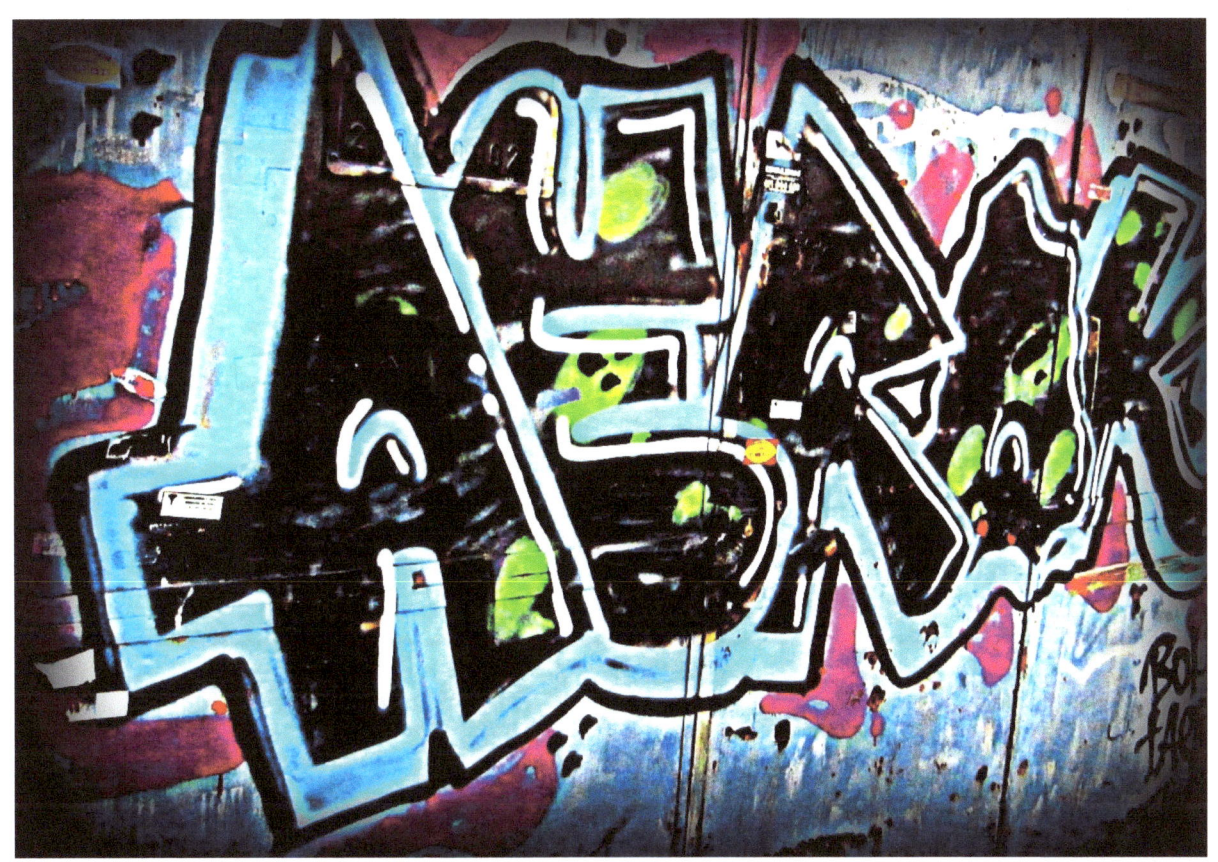

Graffiti, Madrid

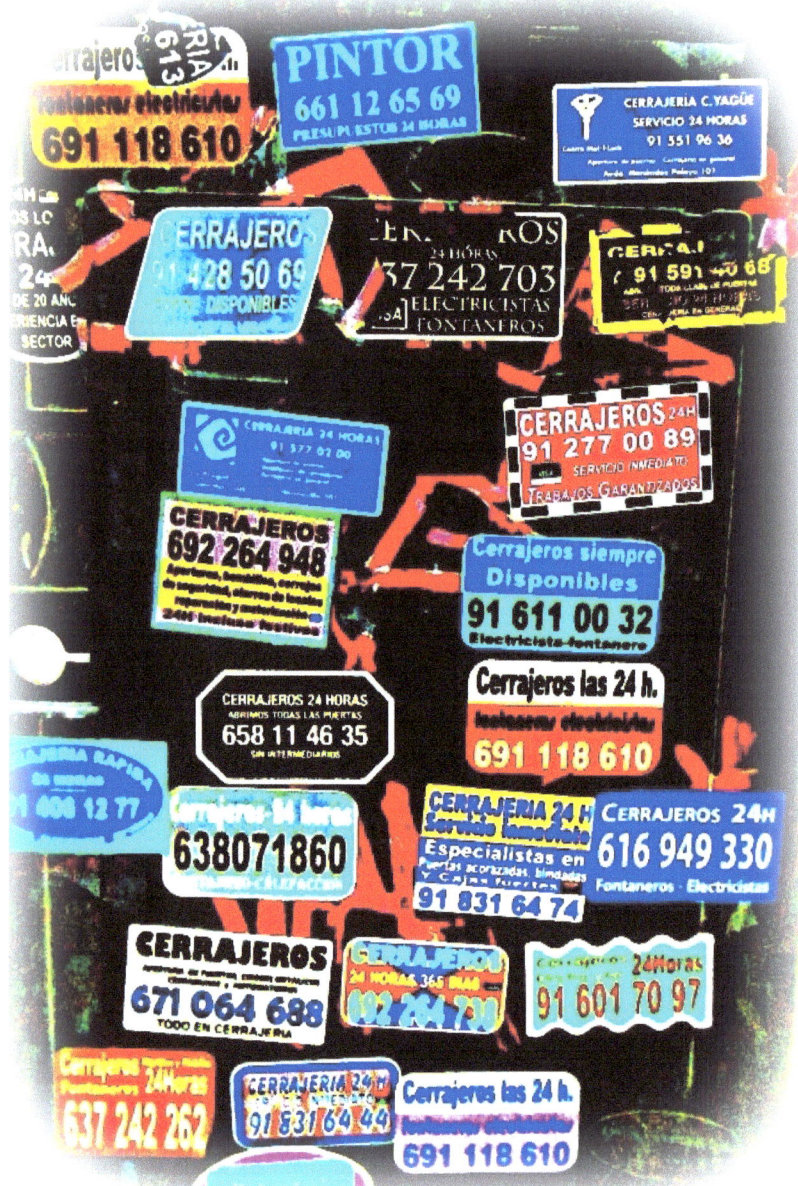

No Bill Posters

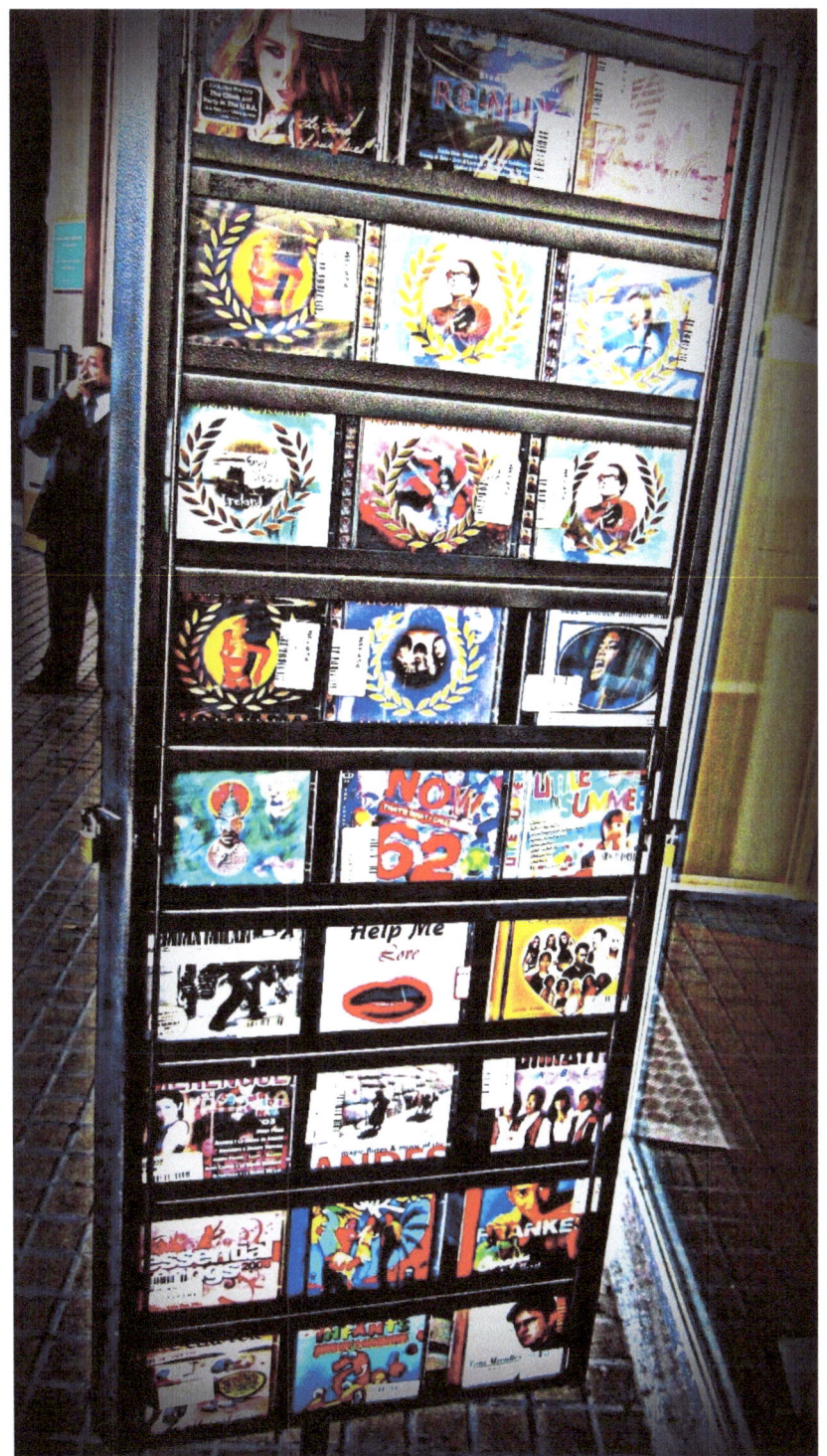

Spotting Alfred Hitchcock

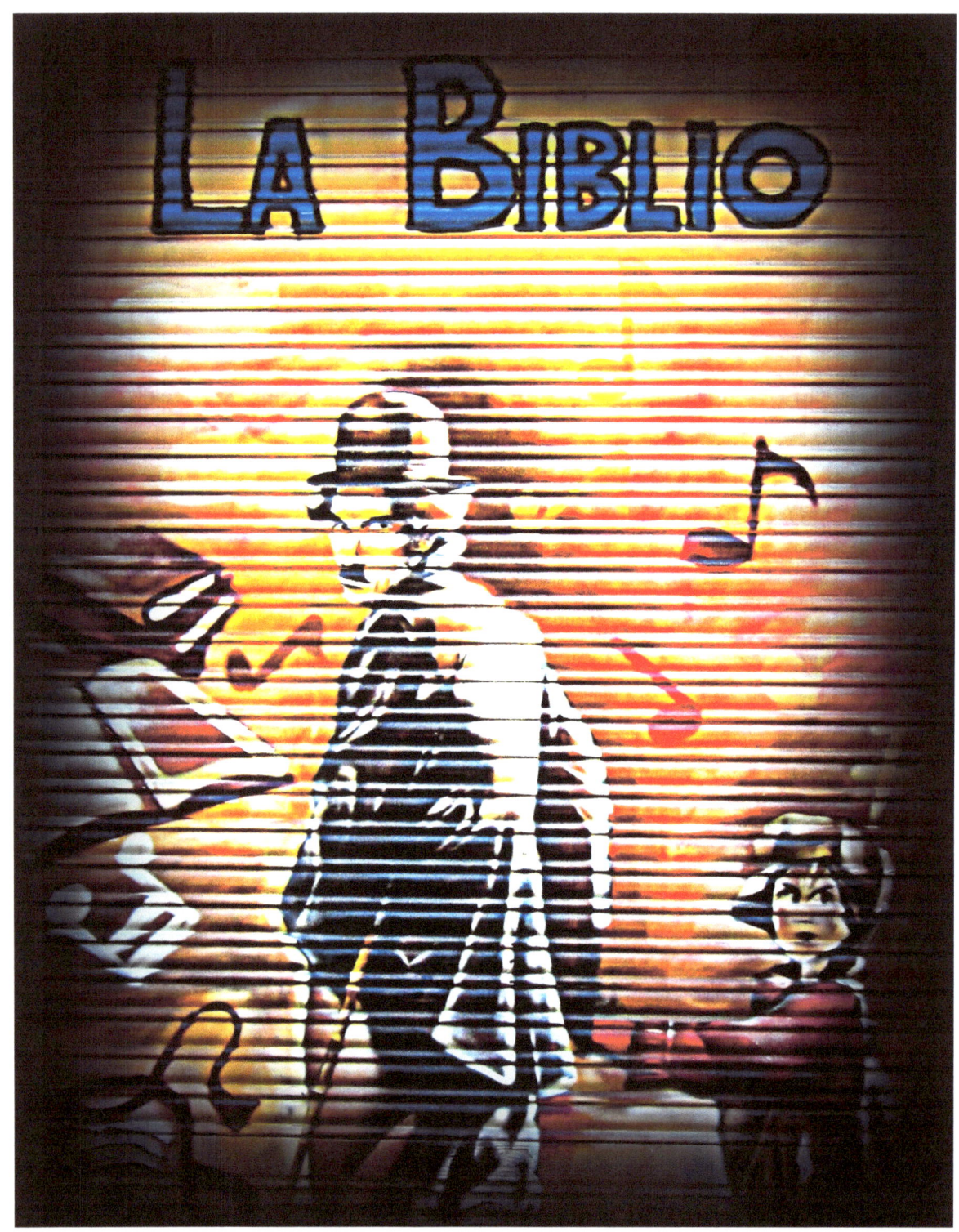

Charlie

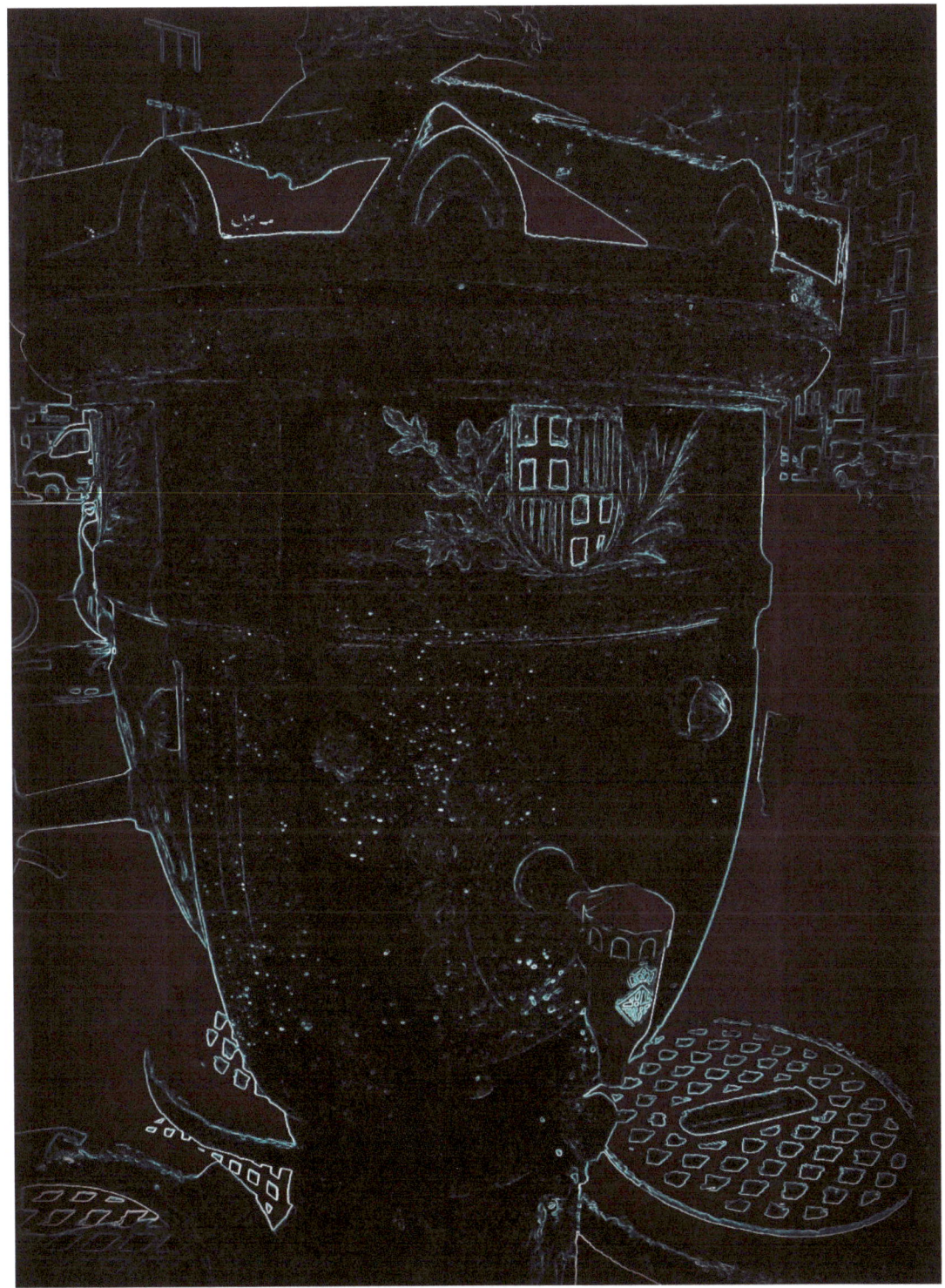

Water Fountain I, Madrid

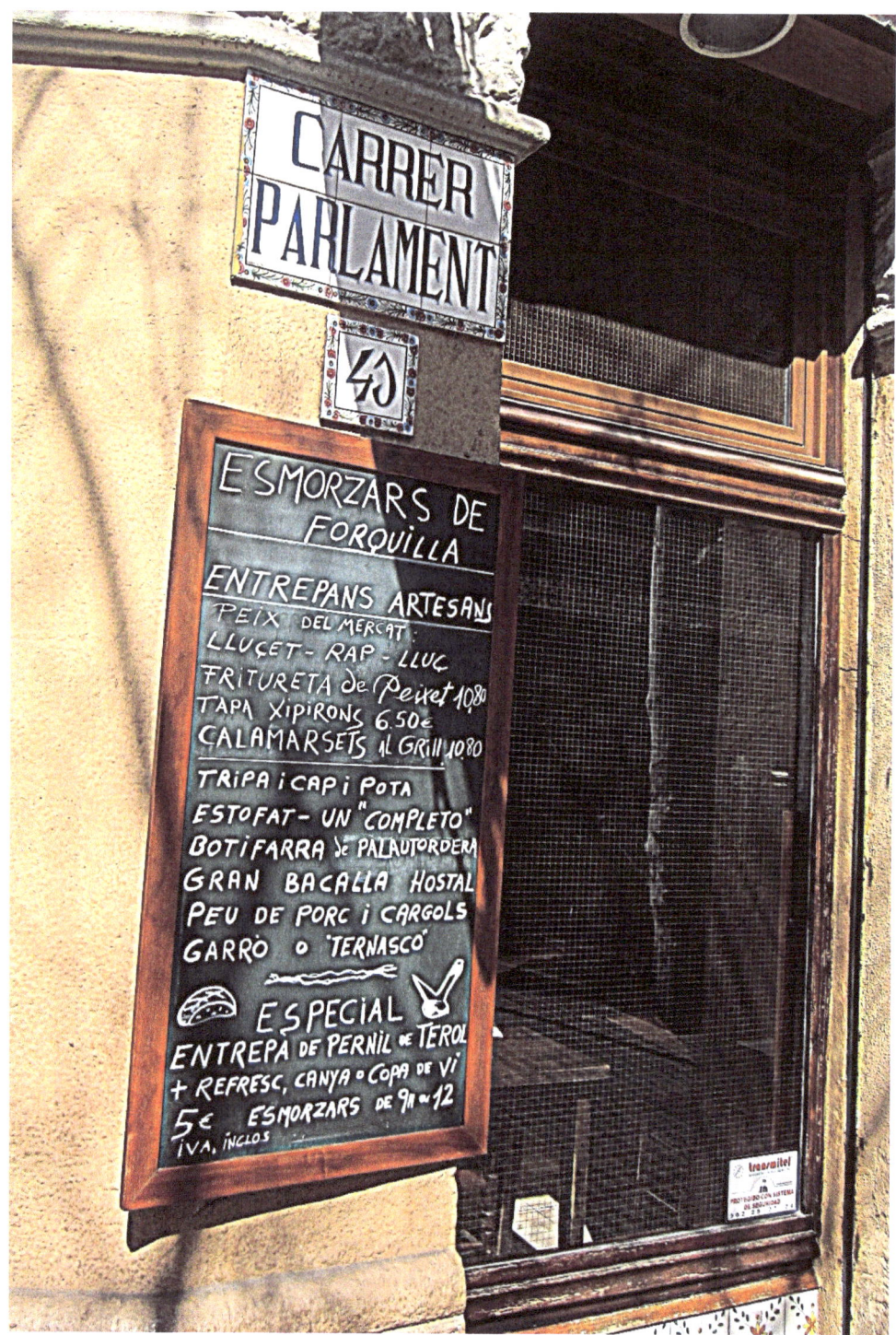

Time for Lunch

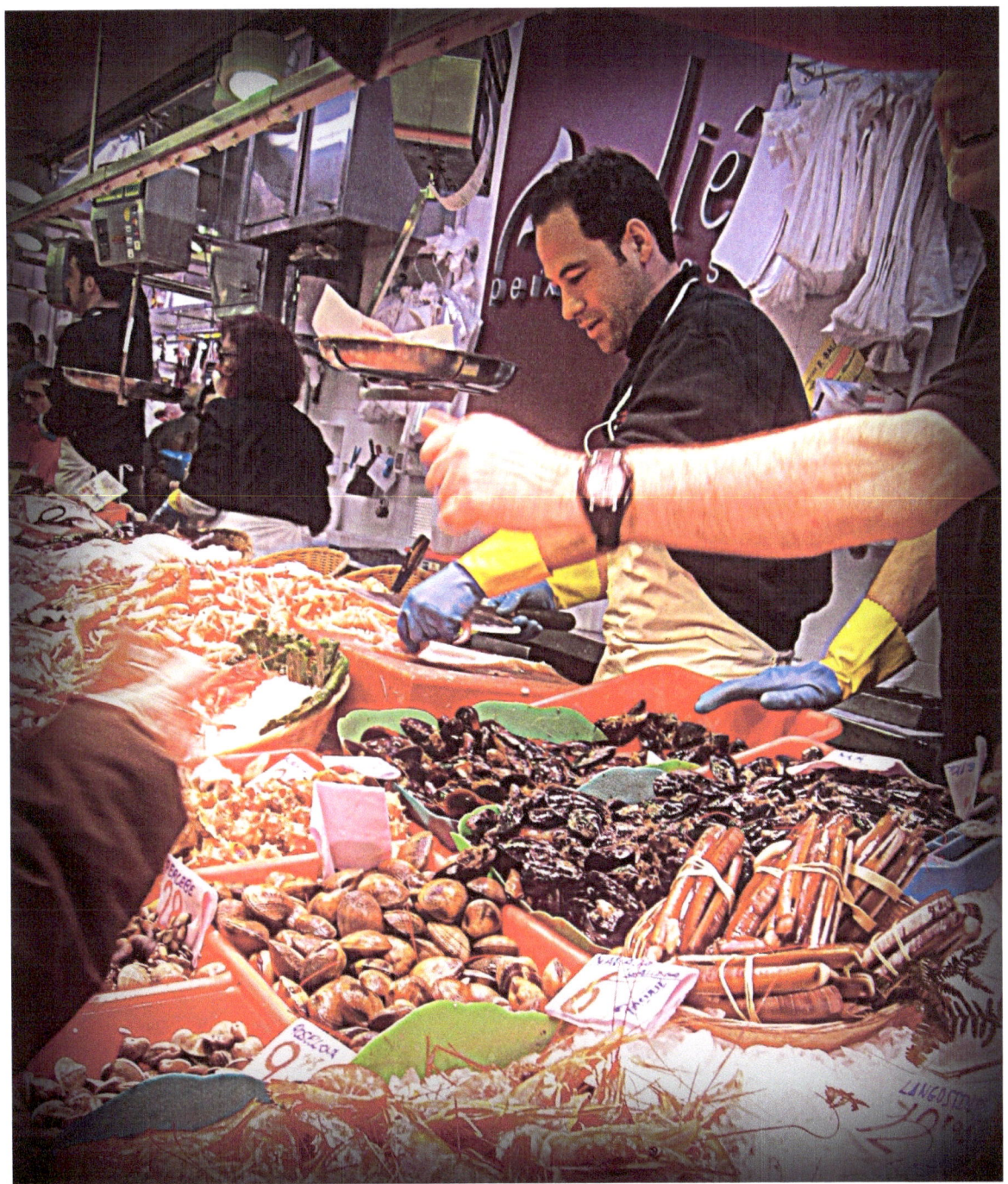

Fish Market

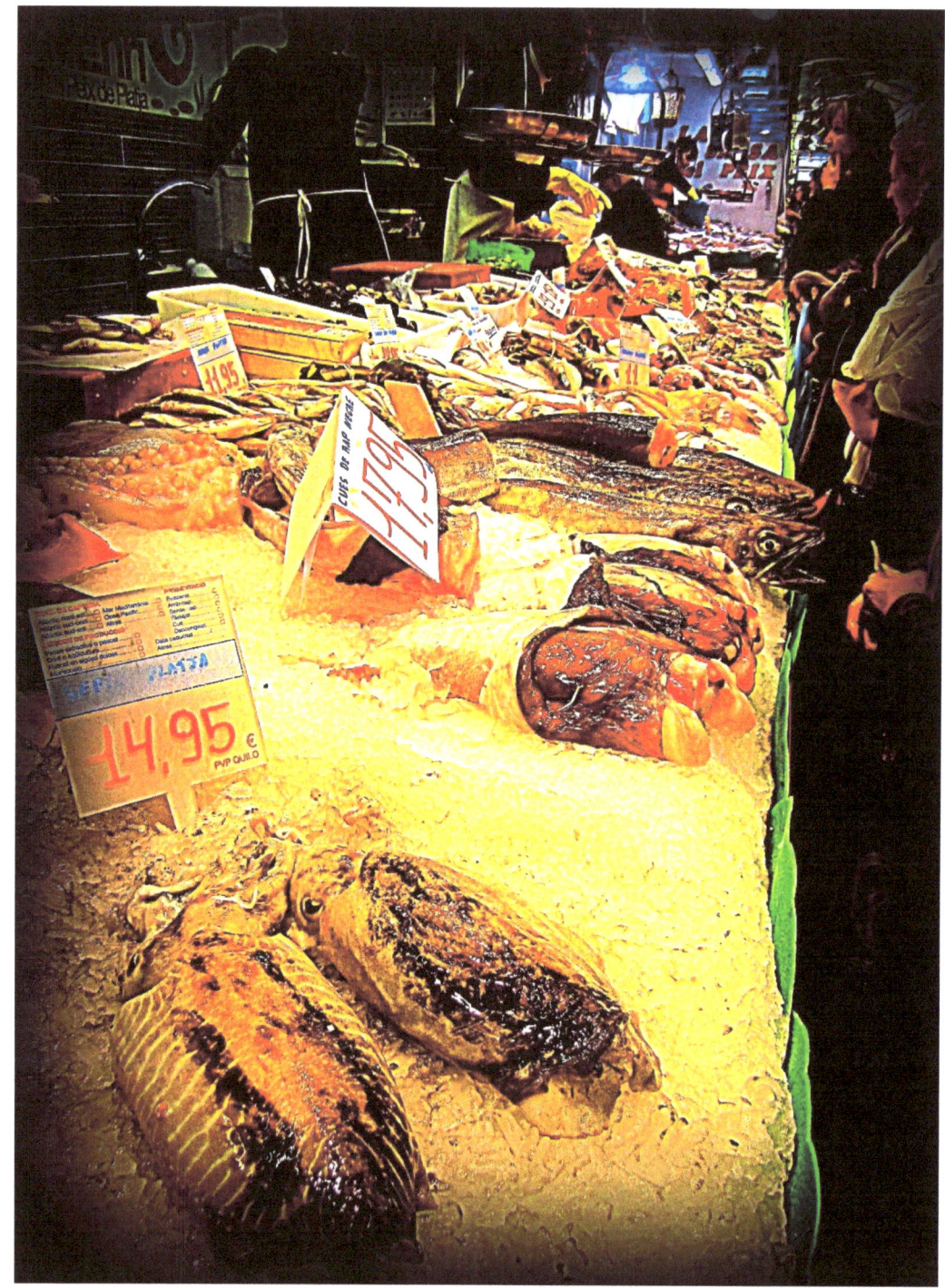

Catch of the Day

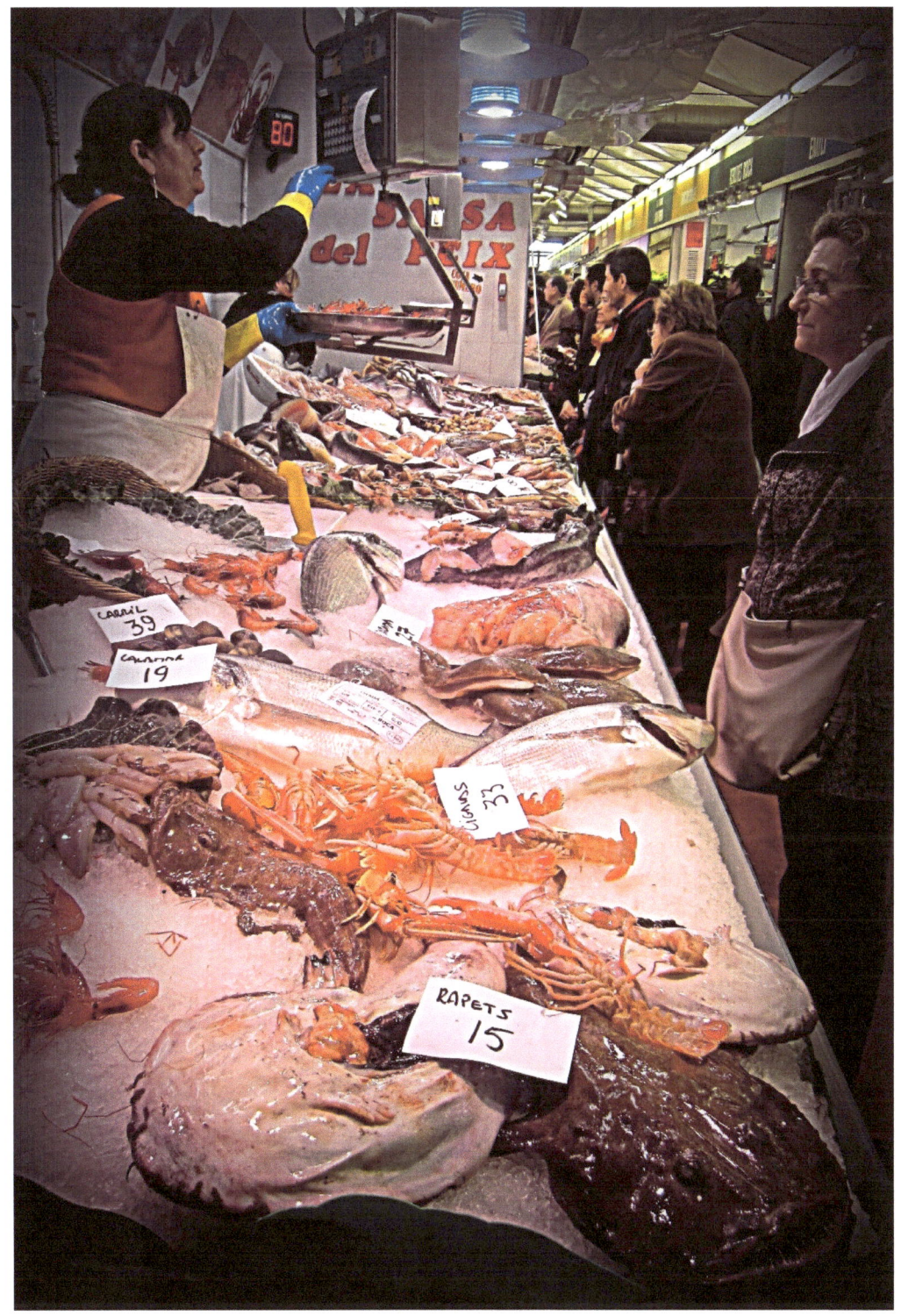

Next!

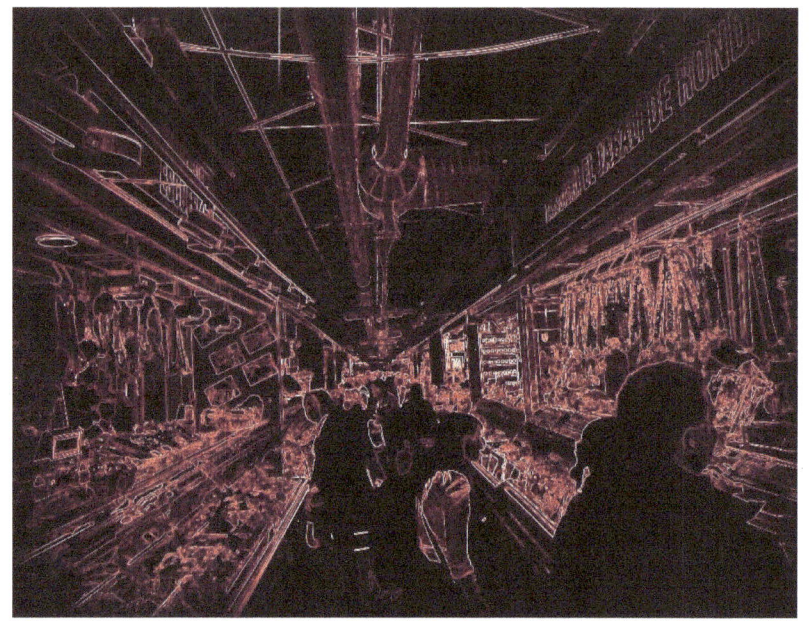

Meat Market

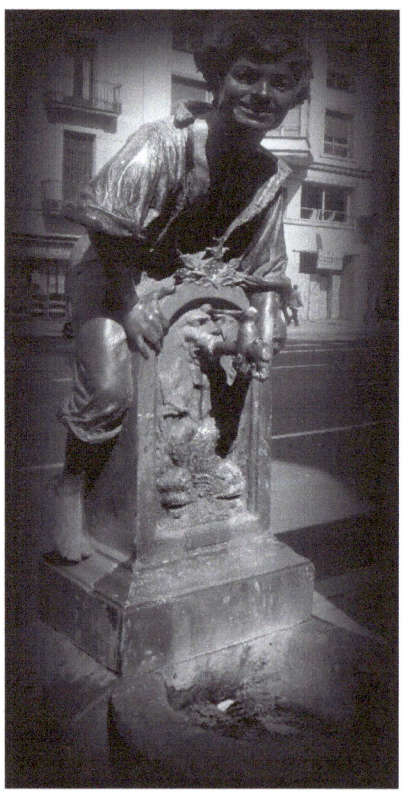

Water Fountain II

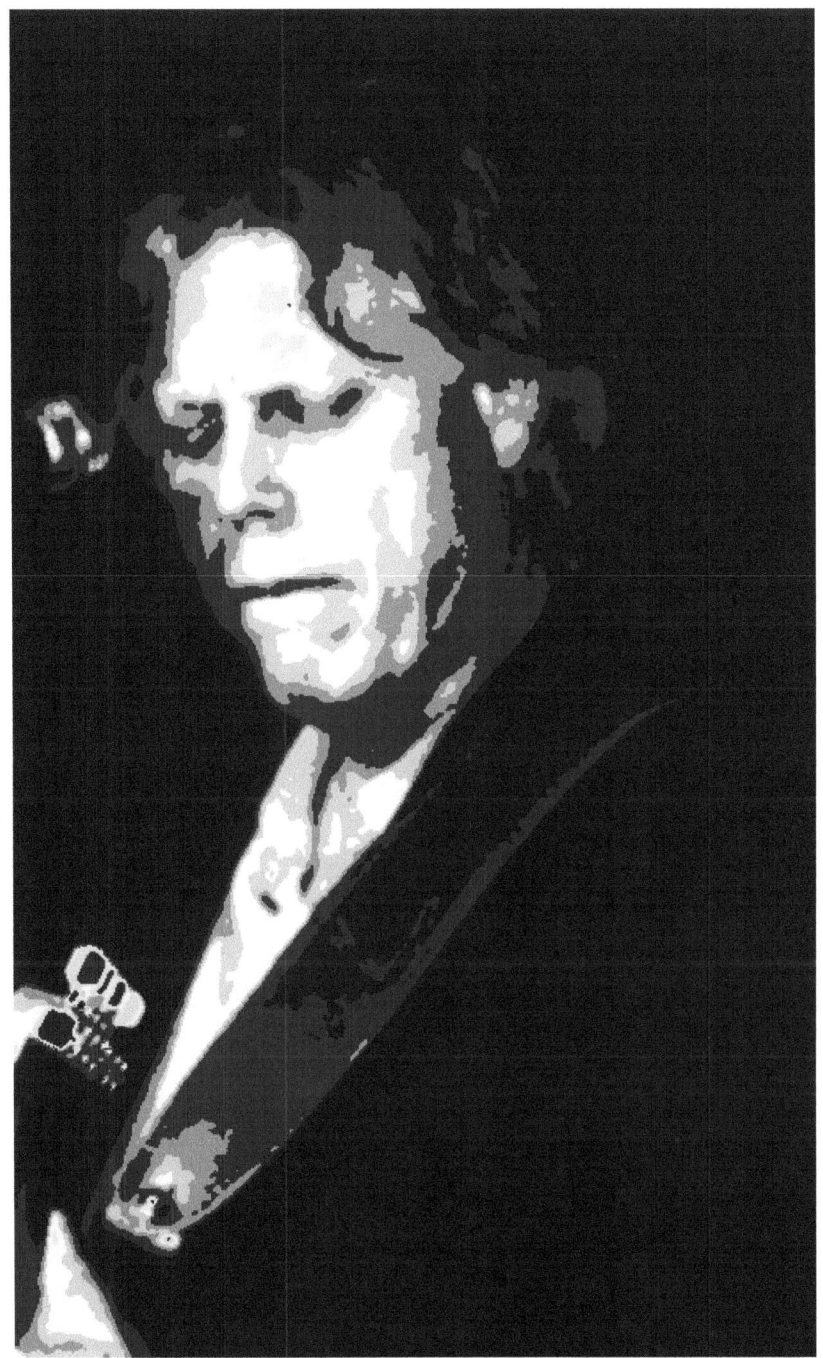

Tom Bowling

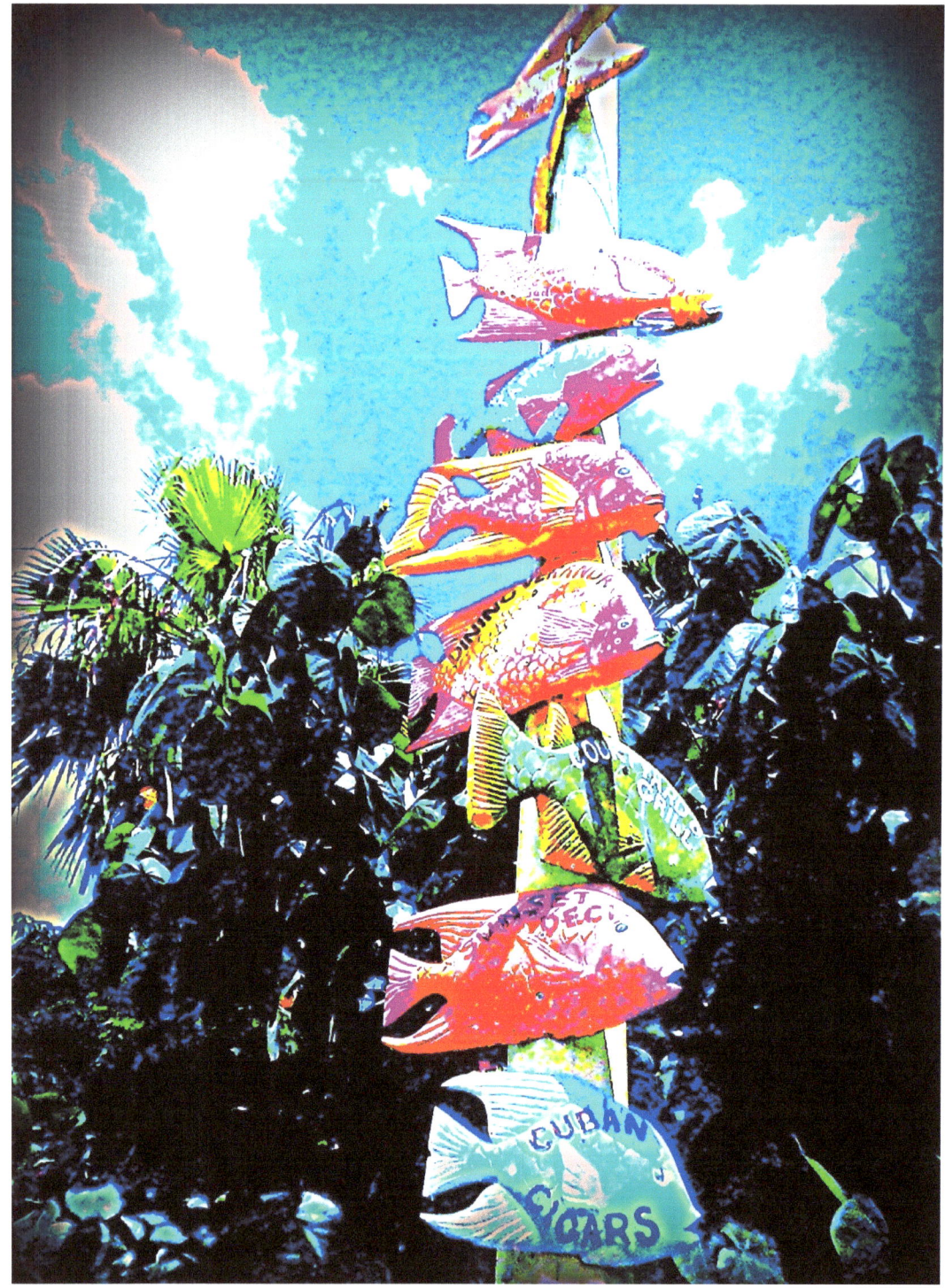

Fish Stick

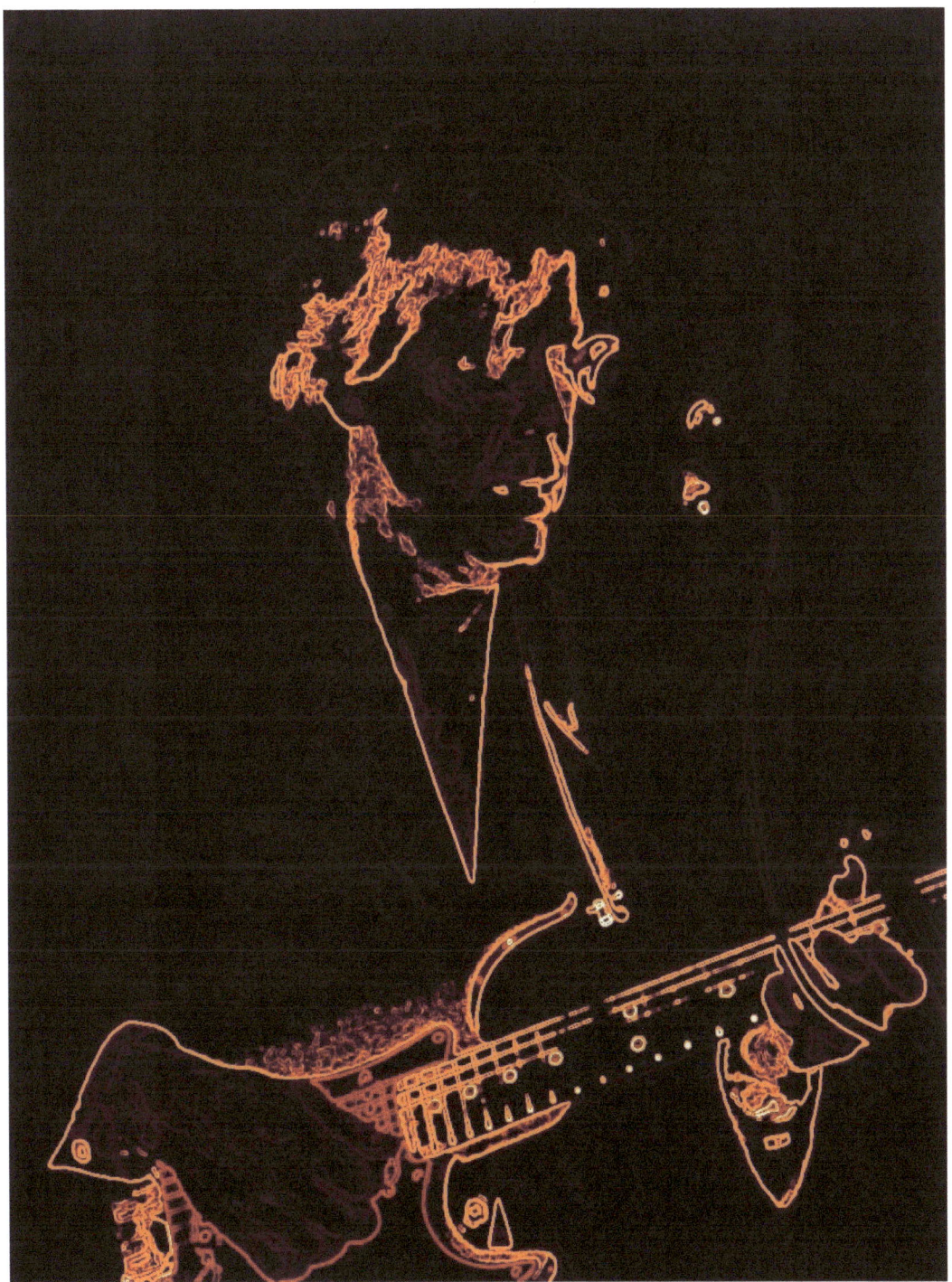

Tom Bowling II

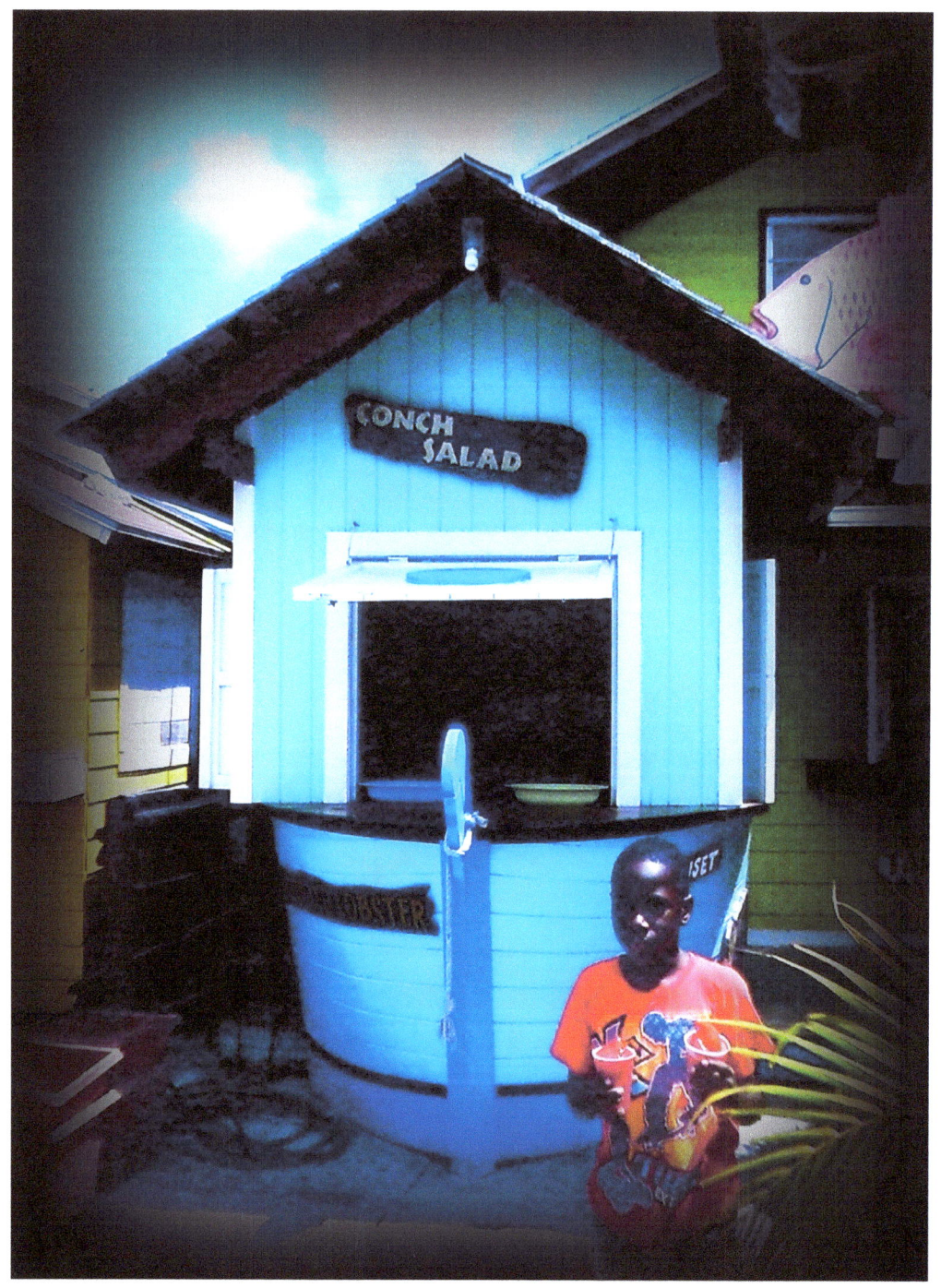

Salad Days with Conch

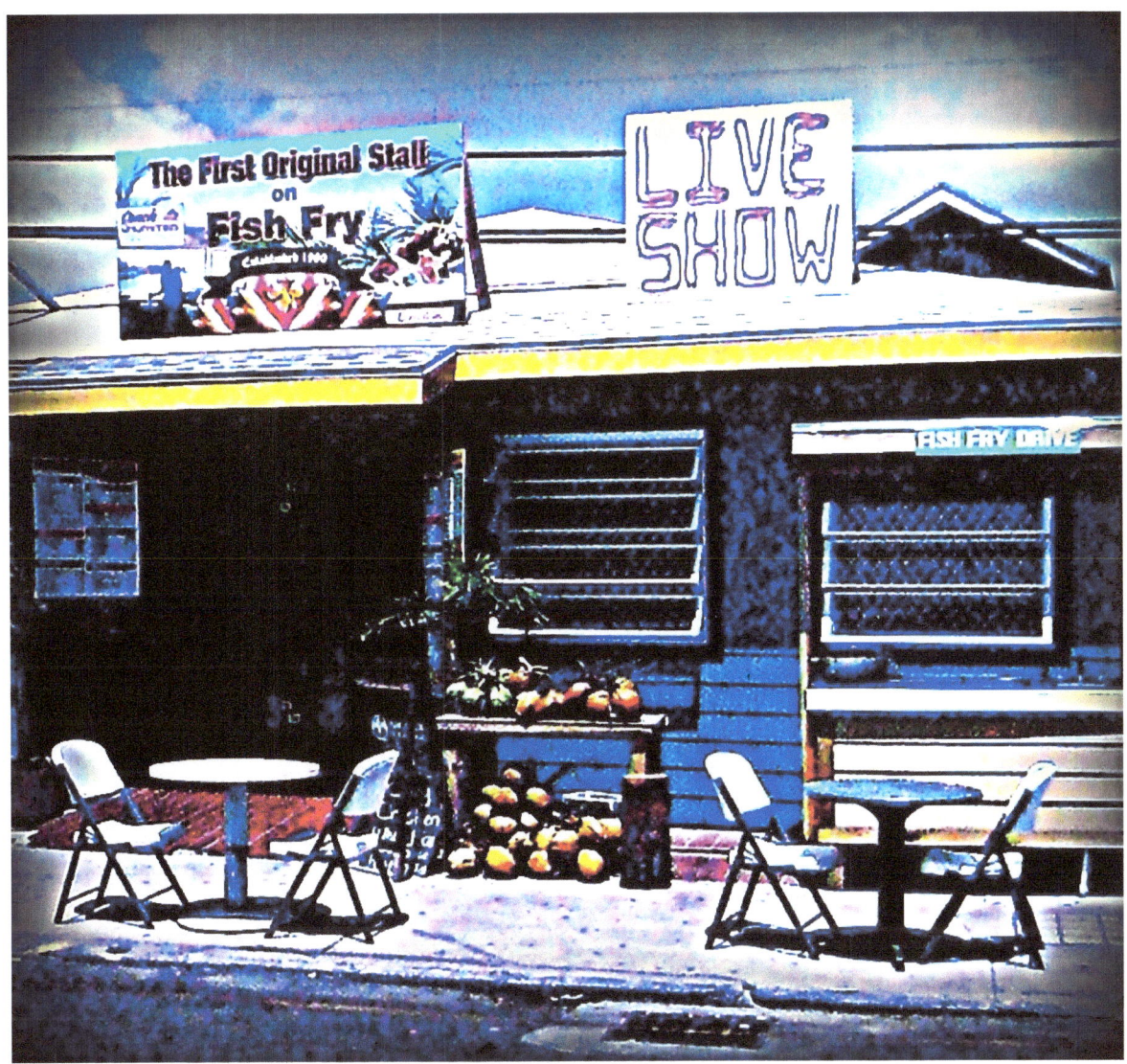

Live Fish Fry

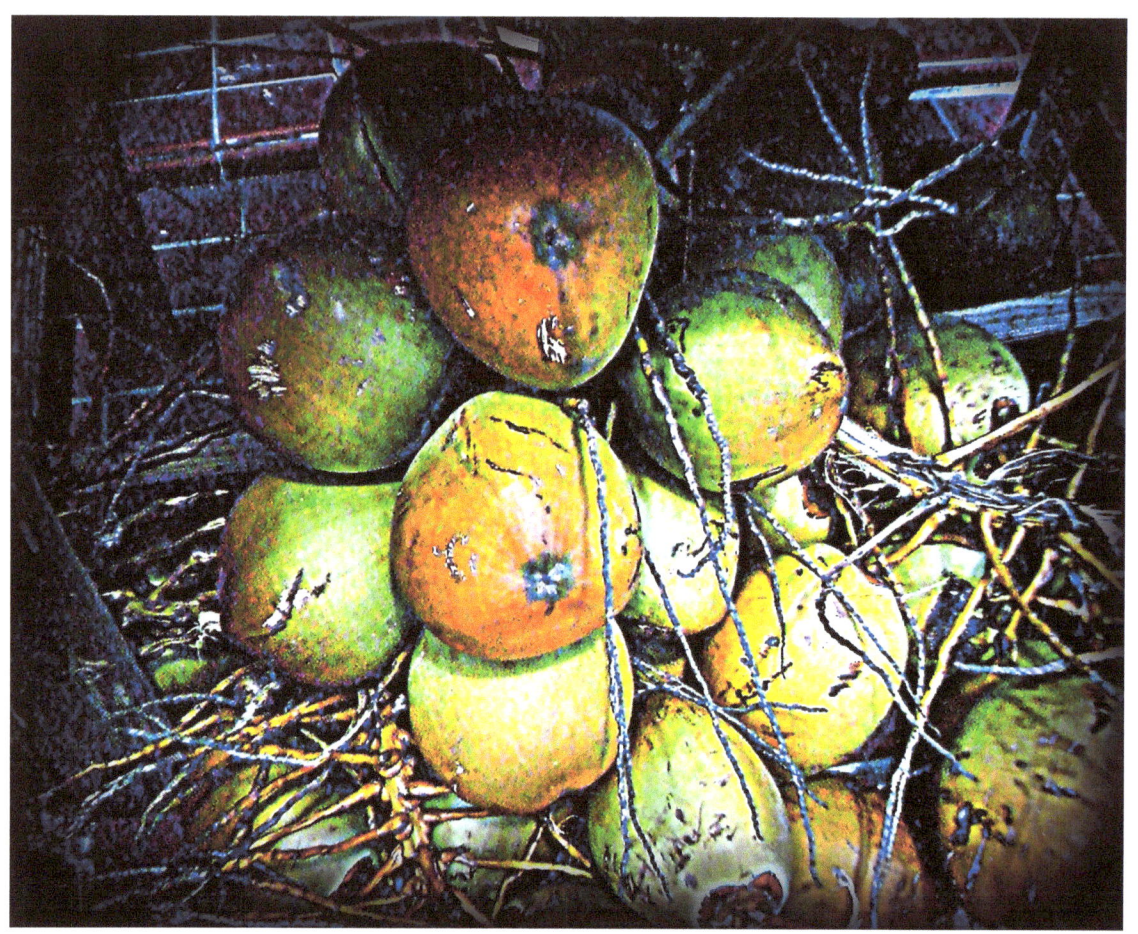

Fruit of the Lens

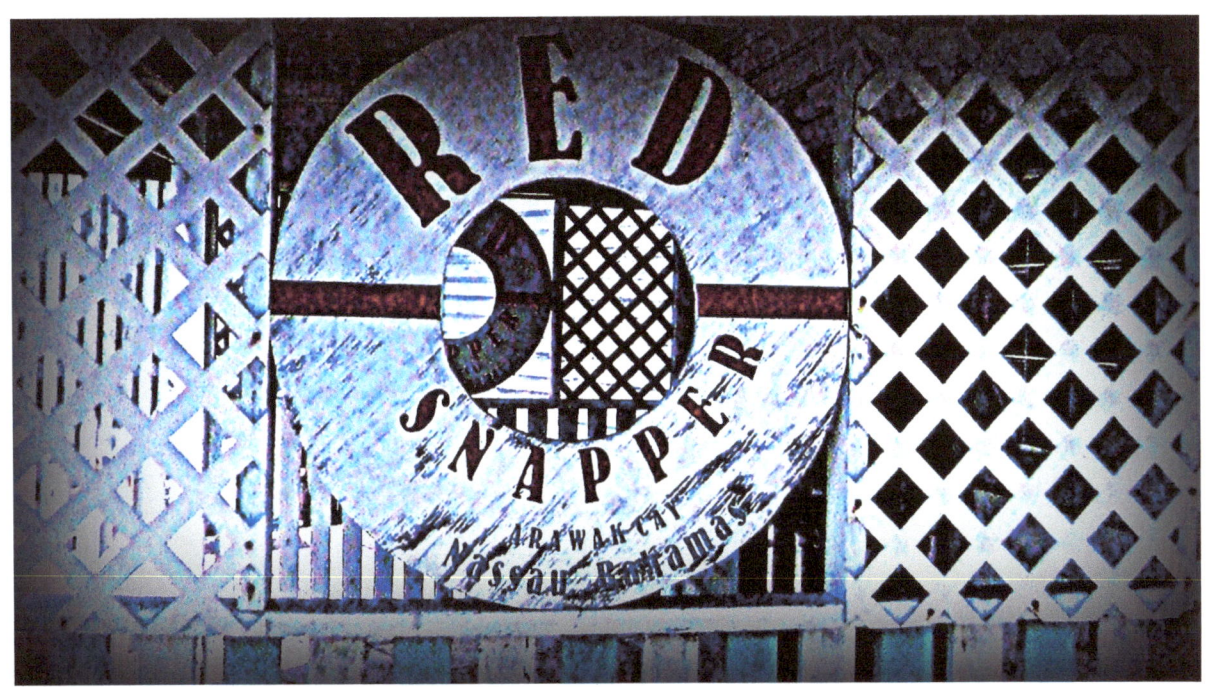

Red Snapper Snap II

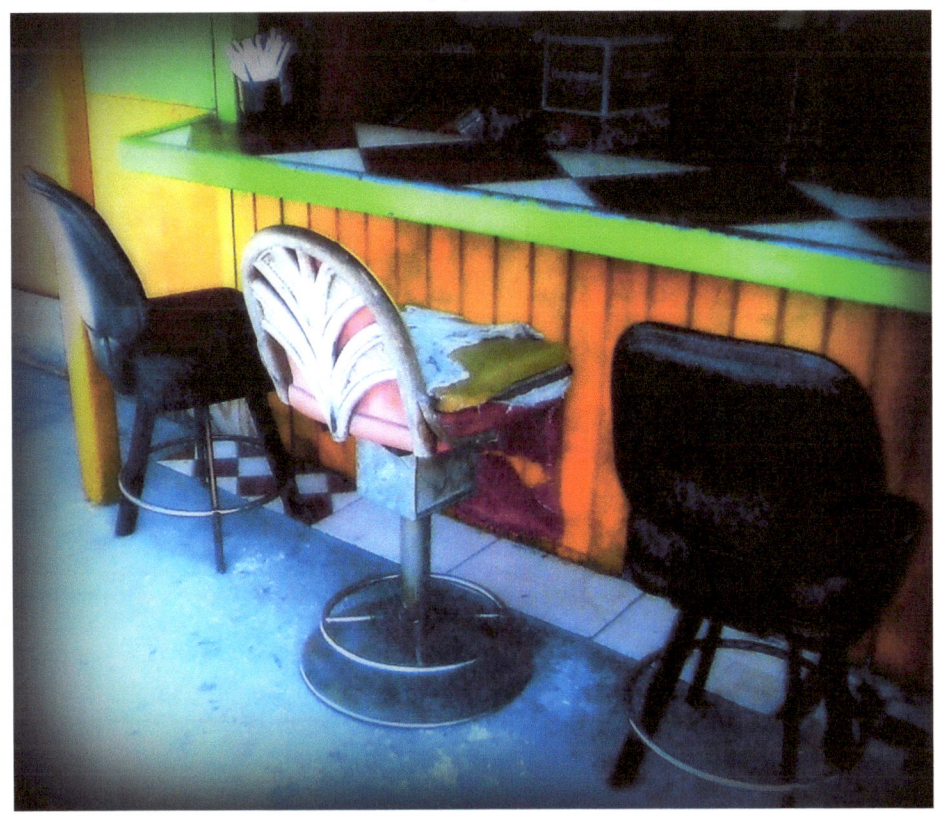

Happy Hour

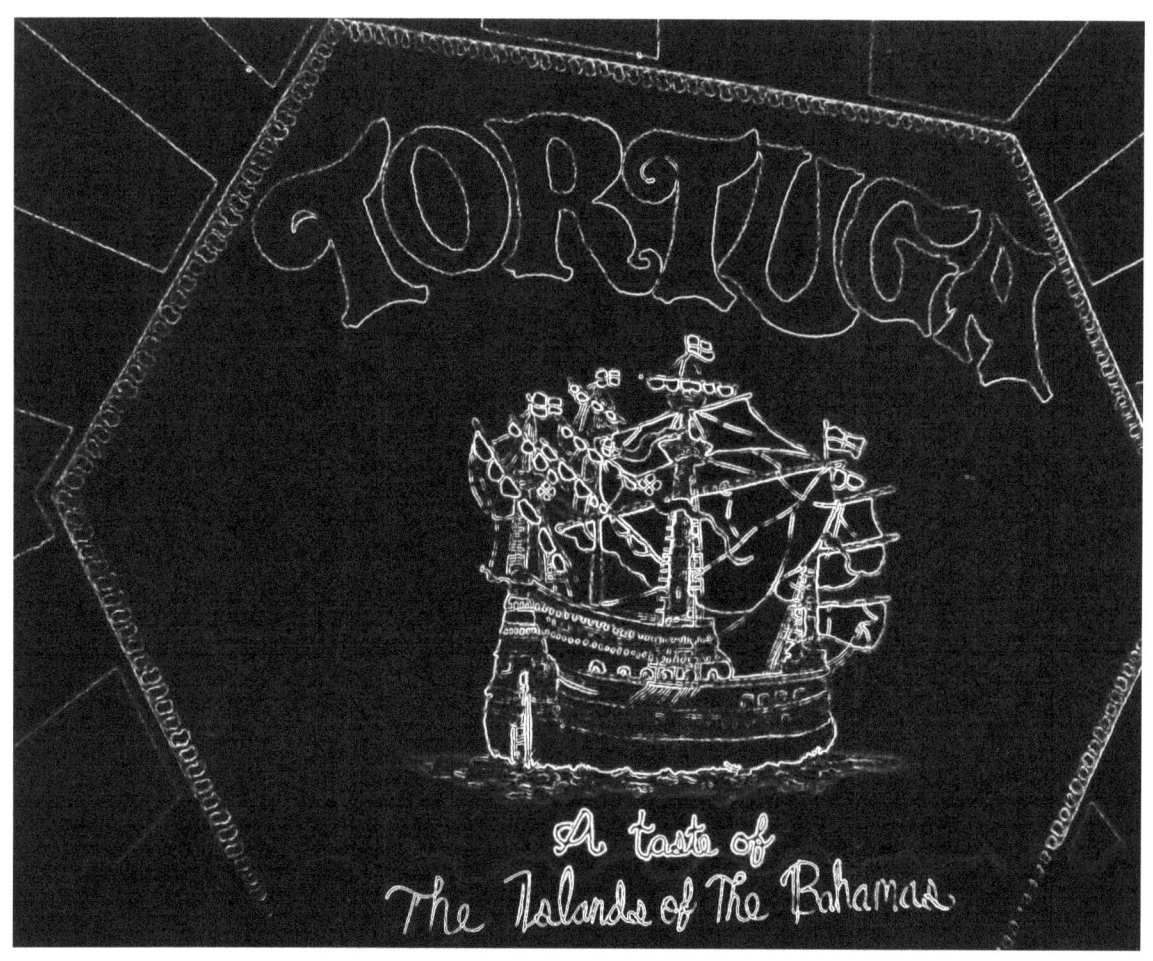

Jolly Roger

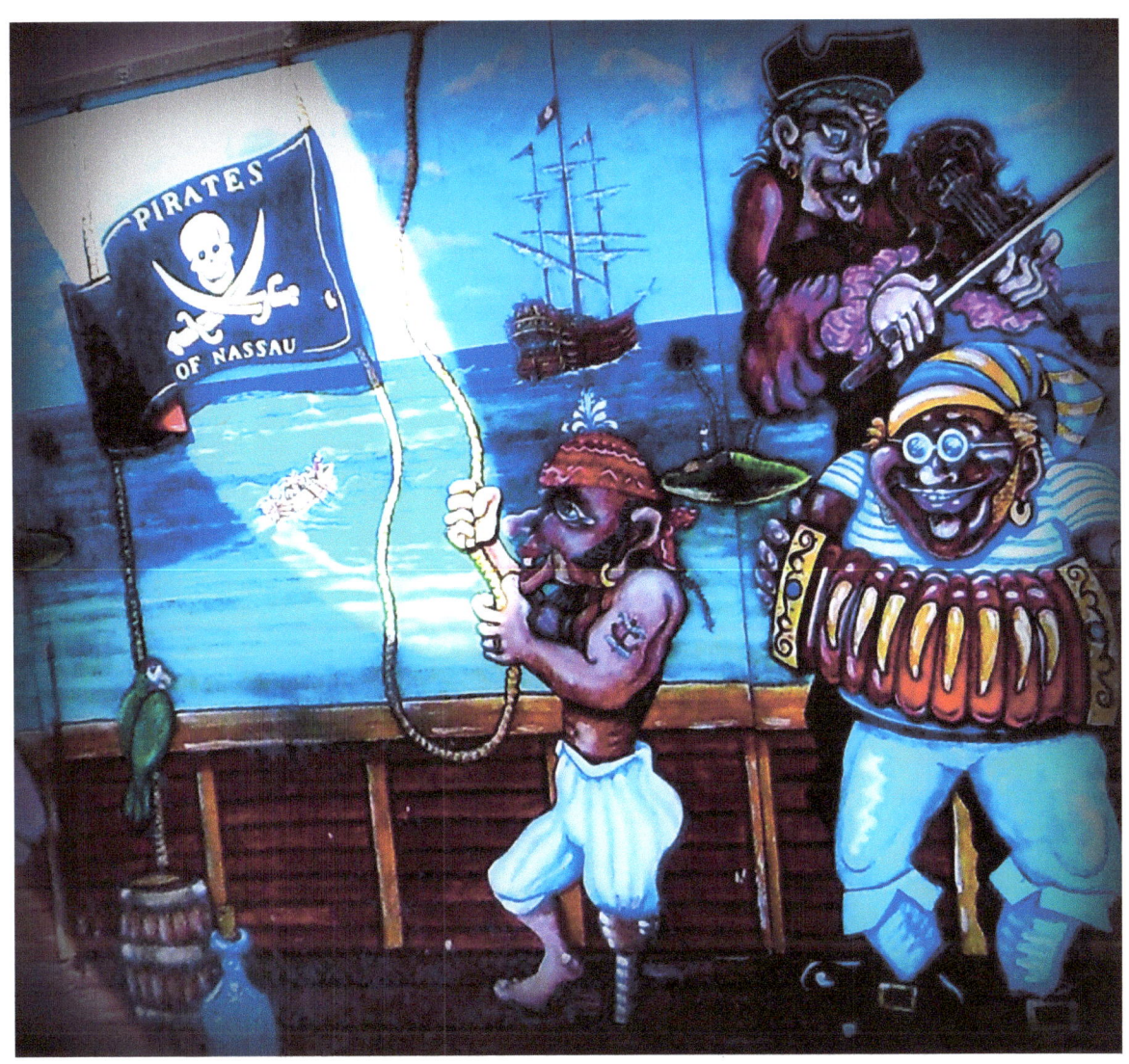

More Pirates of the Caribbean

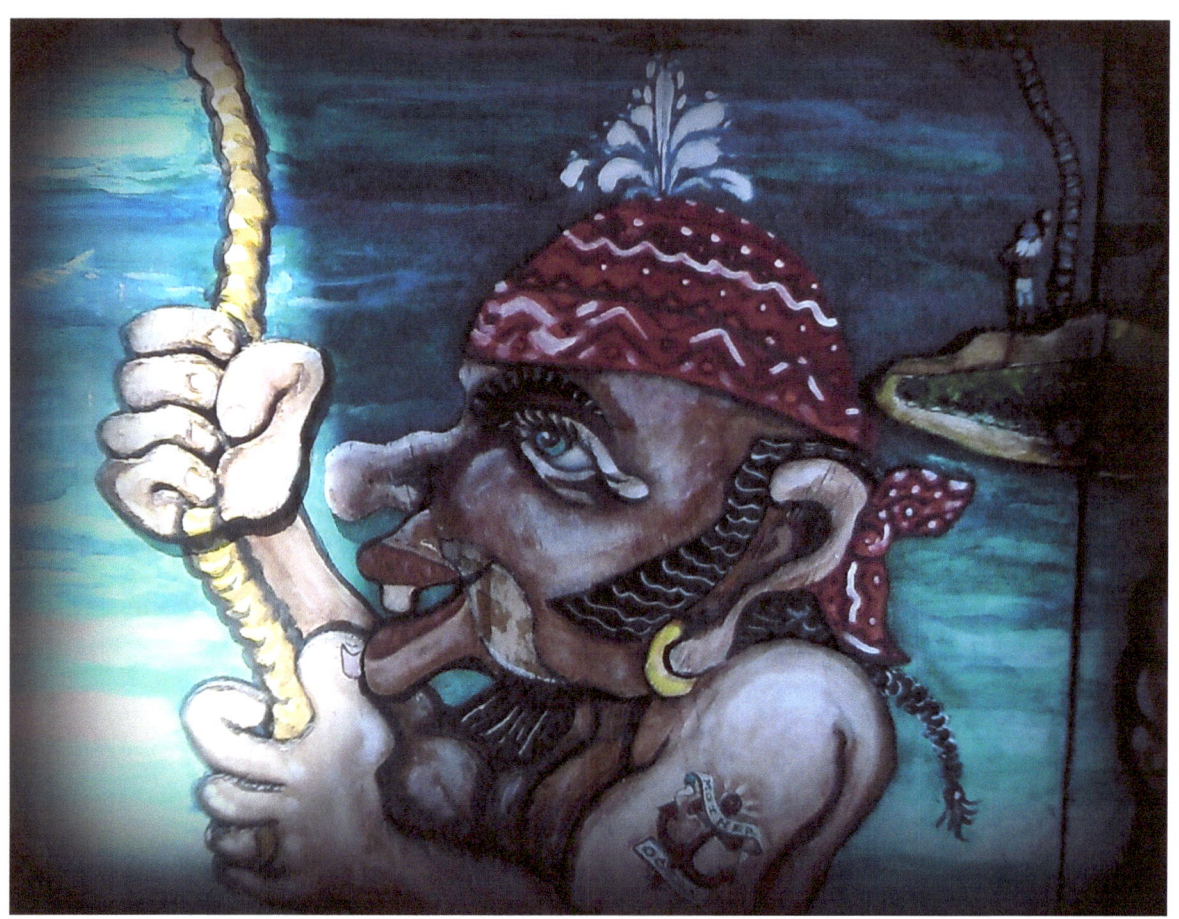

Too Much Grog

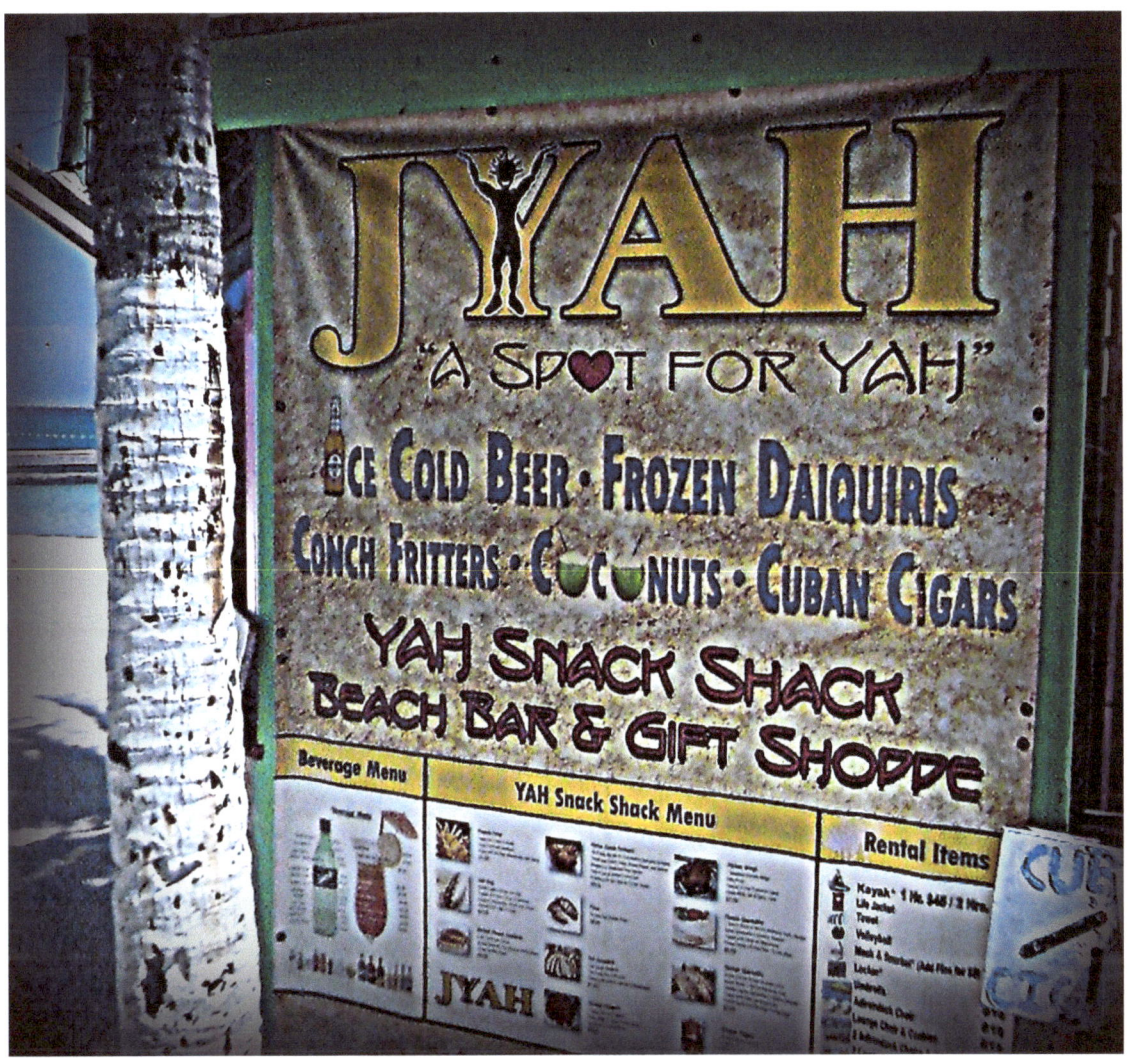

Beach Snacking

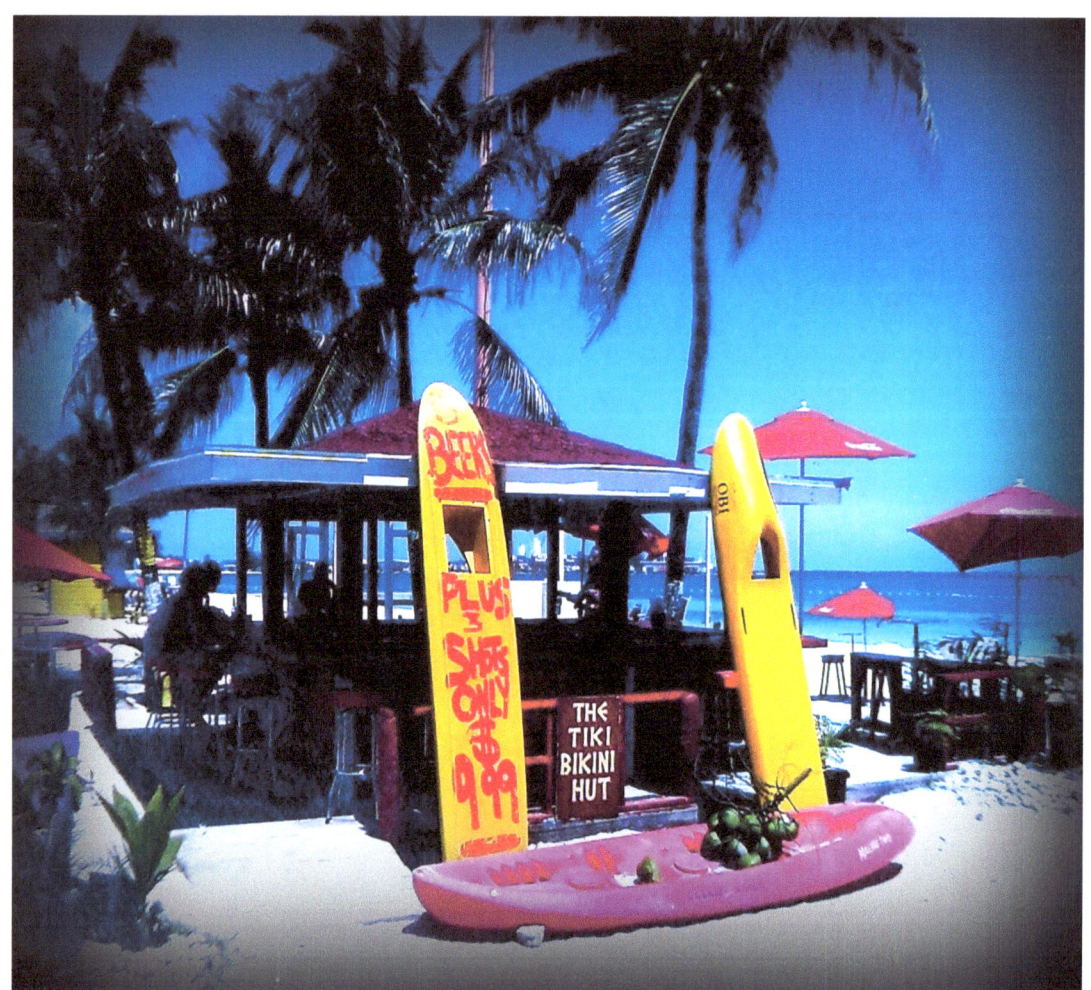

Best Bar None

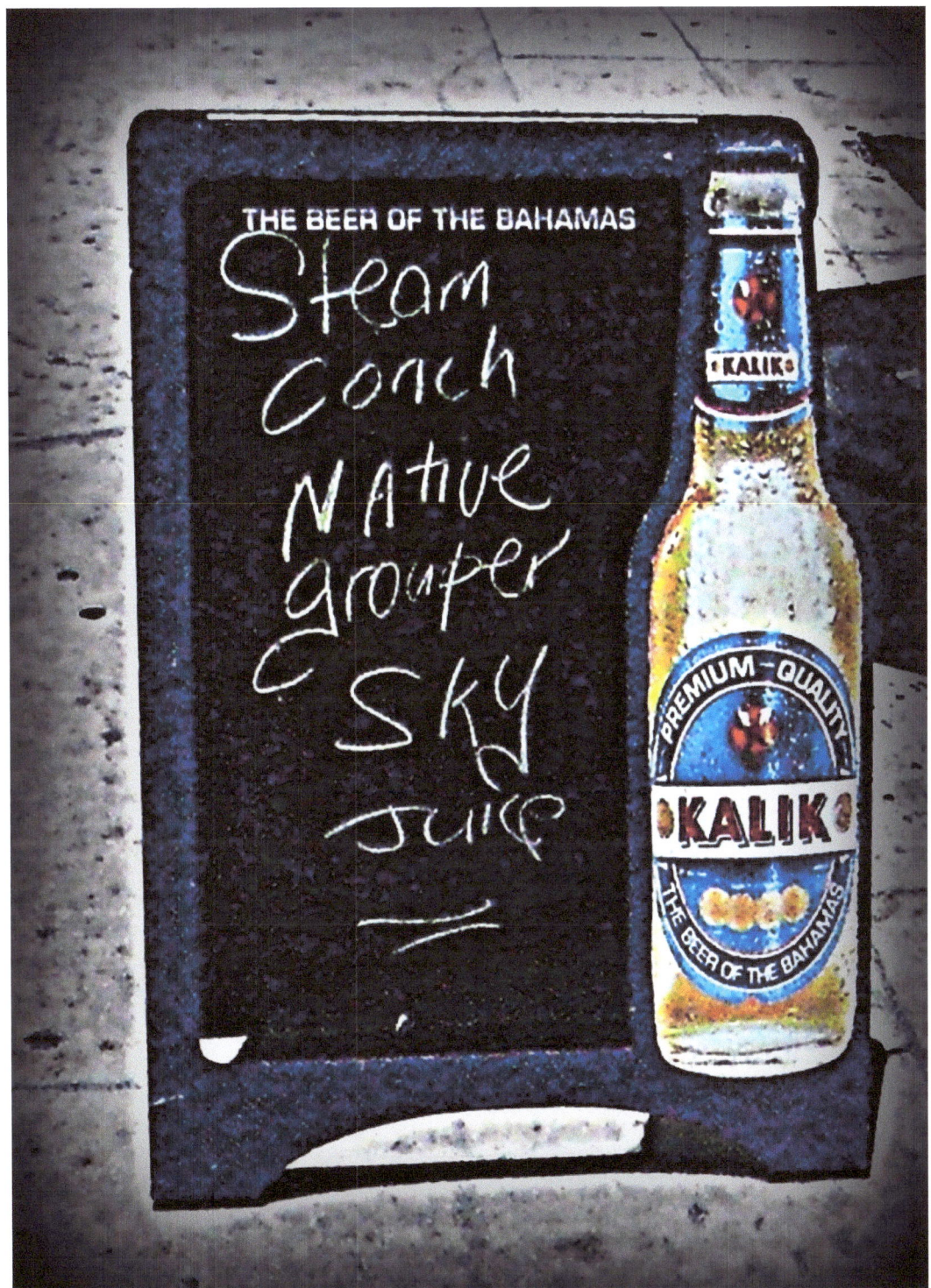

Decisions, Decisions

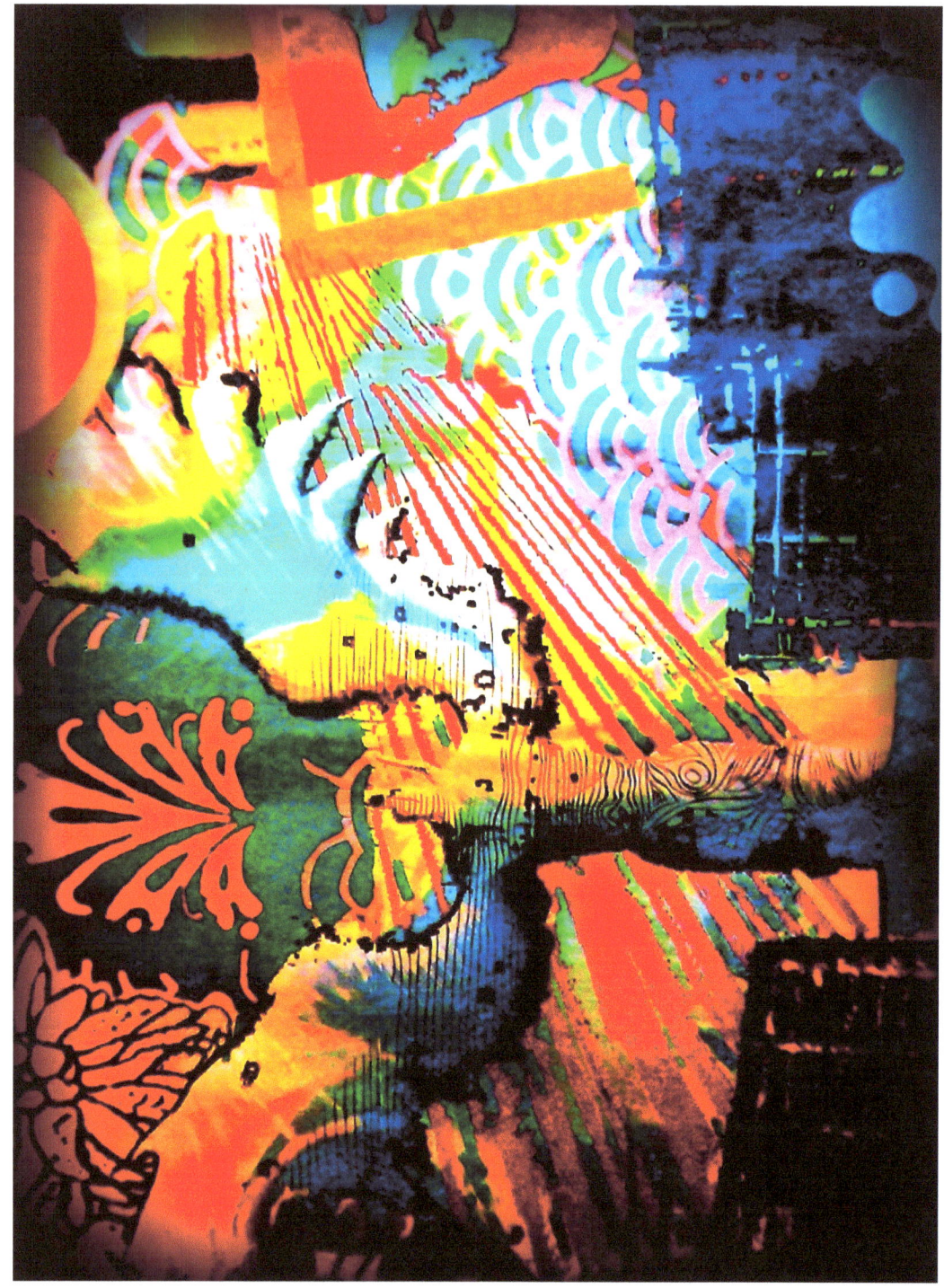

Bahamian Graffiti

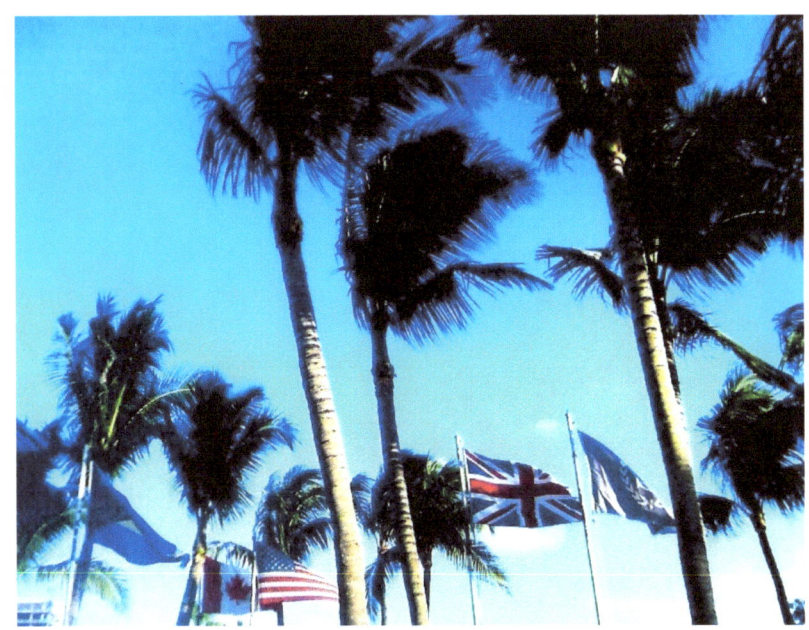

Flying the Flag

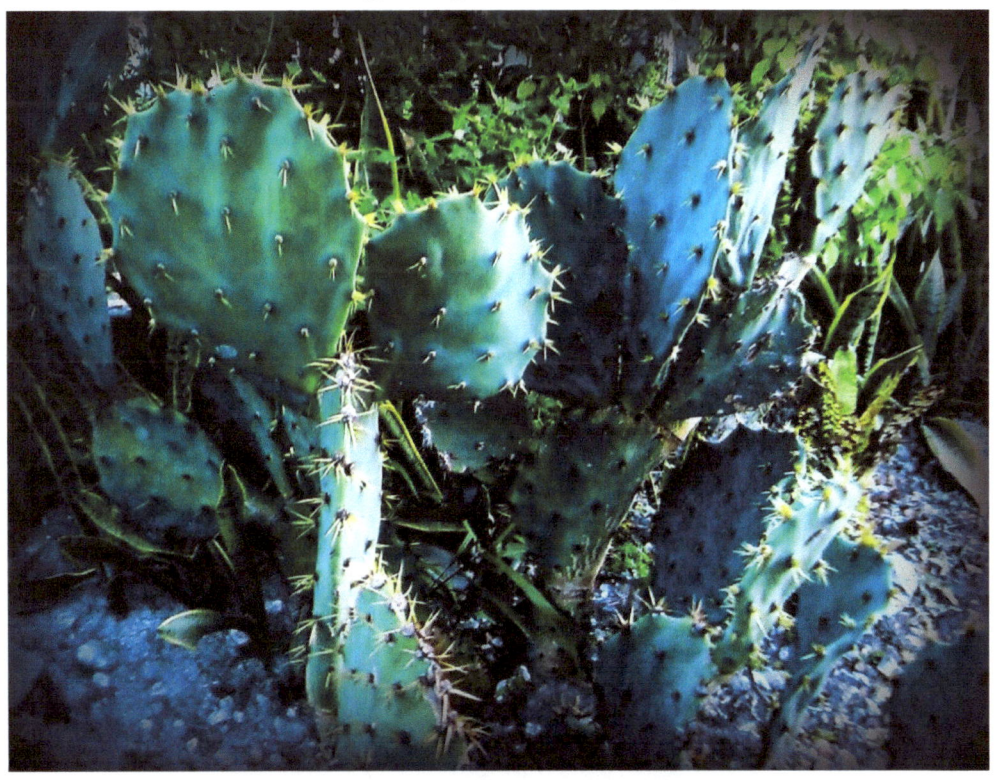

Prickly Business

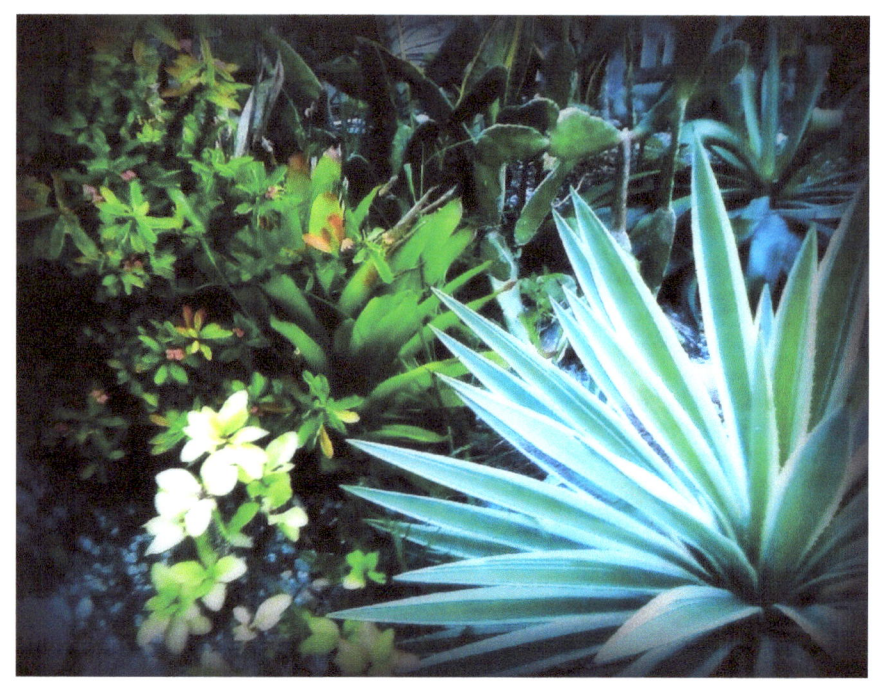

Succulents

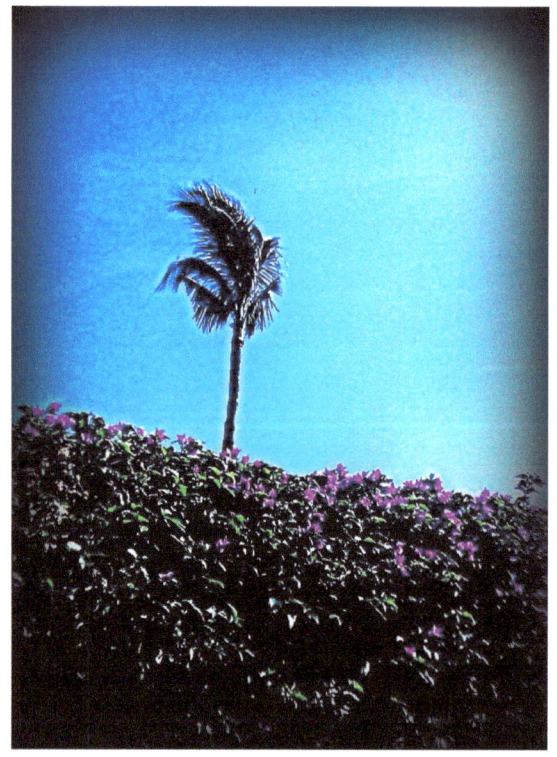

Palm D'or

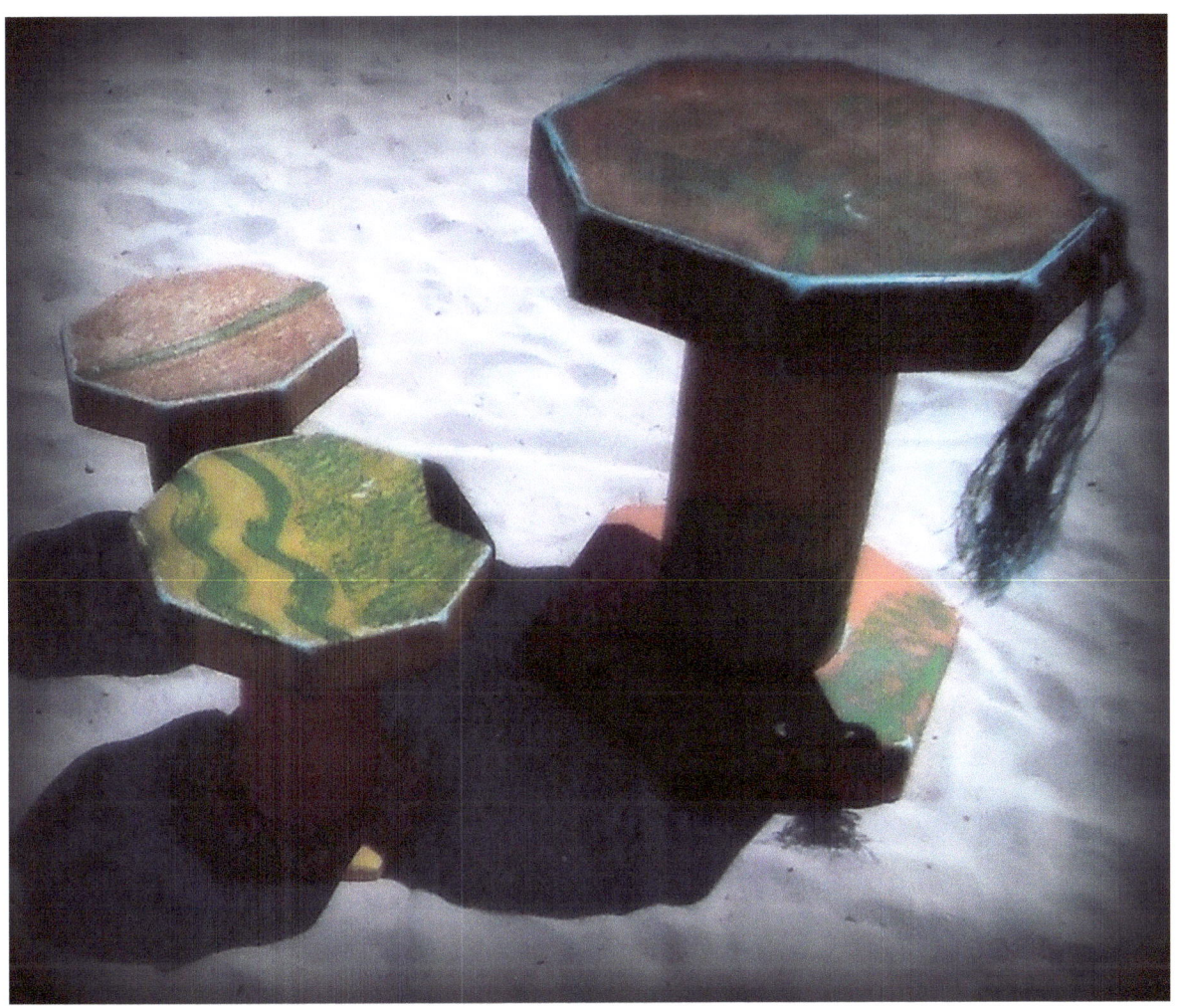

Beach Table and Chairs

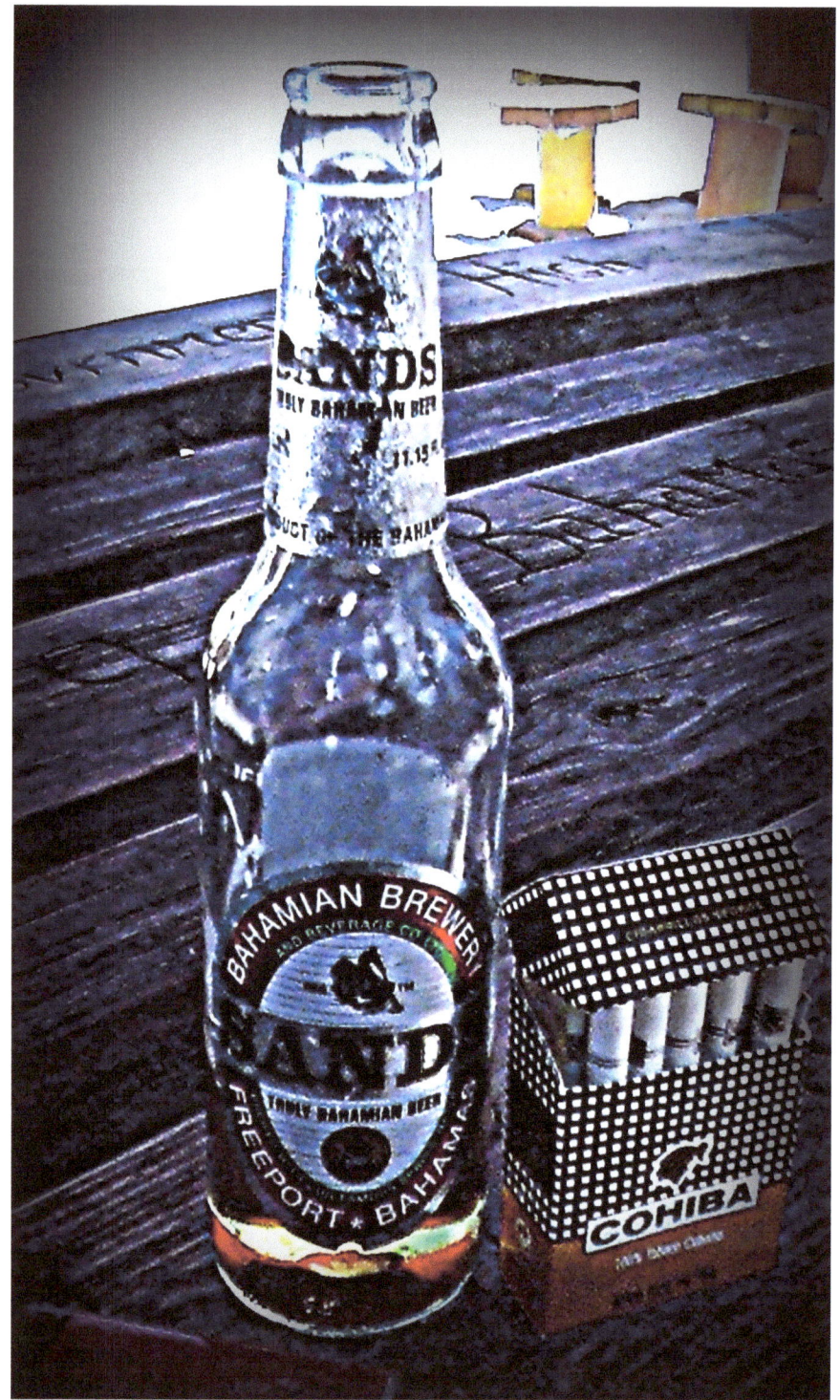

Quick Lunch

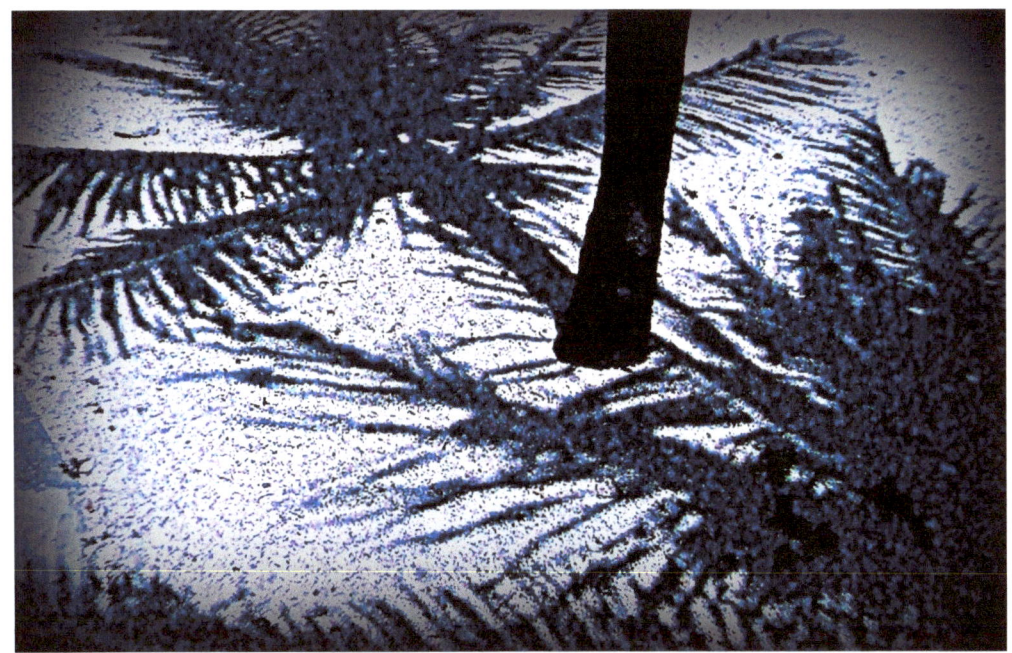

Sand and Shade

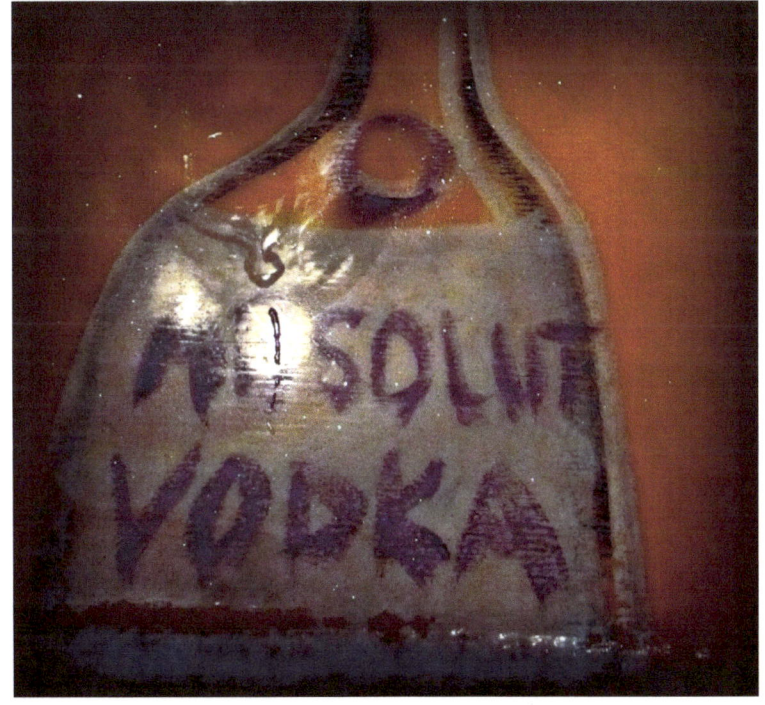

I Will Take Another

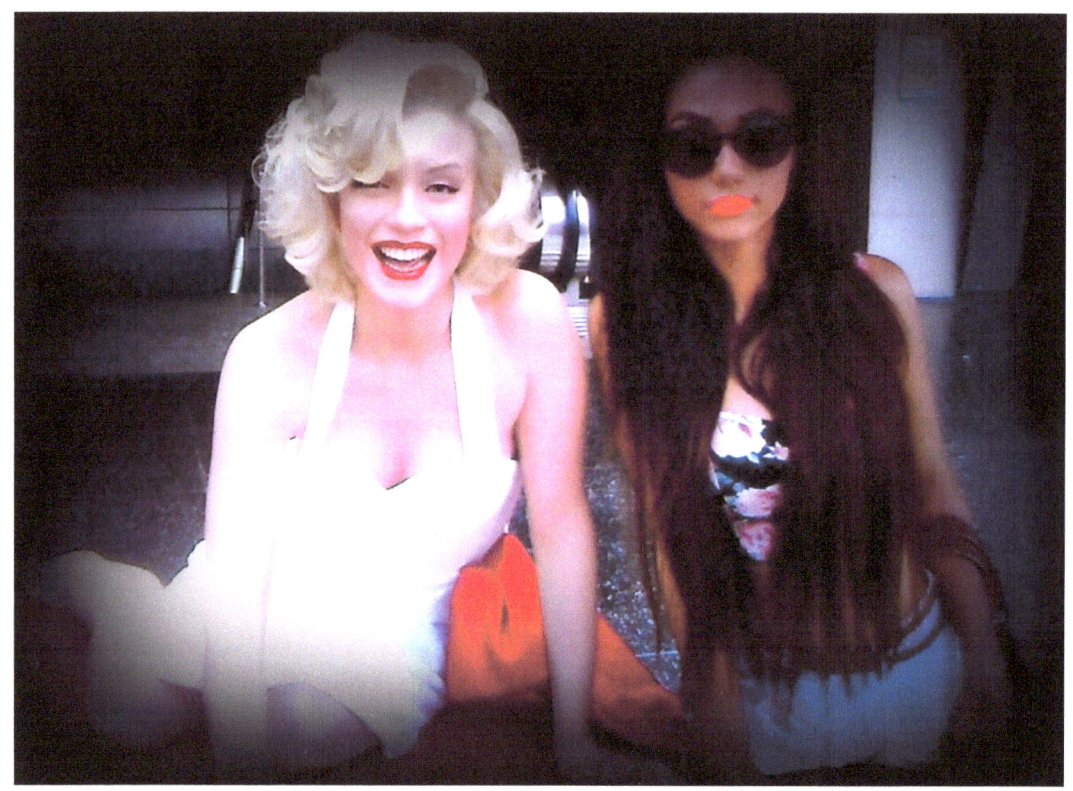

Alex and Marilyn

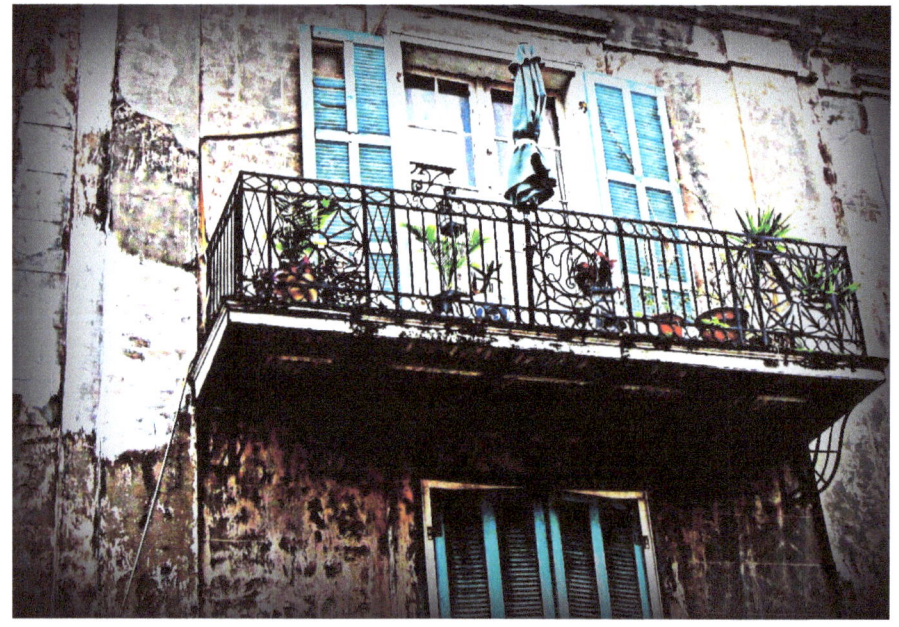

Wherefore Art Thou...?

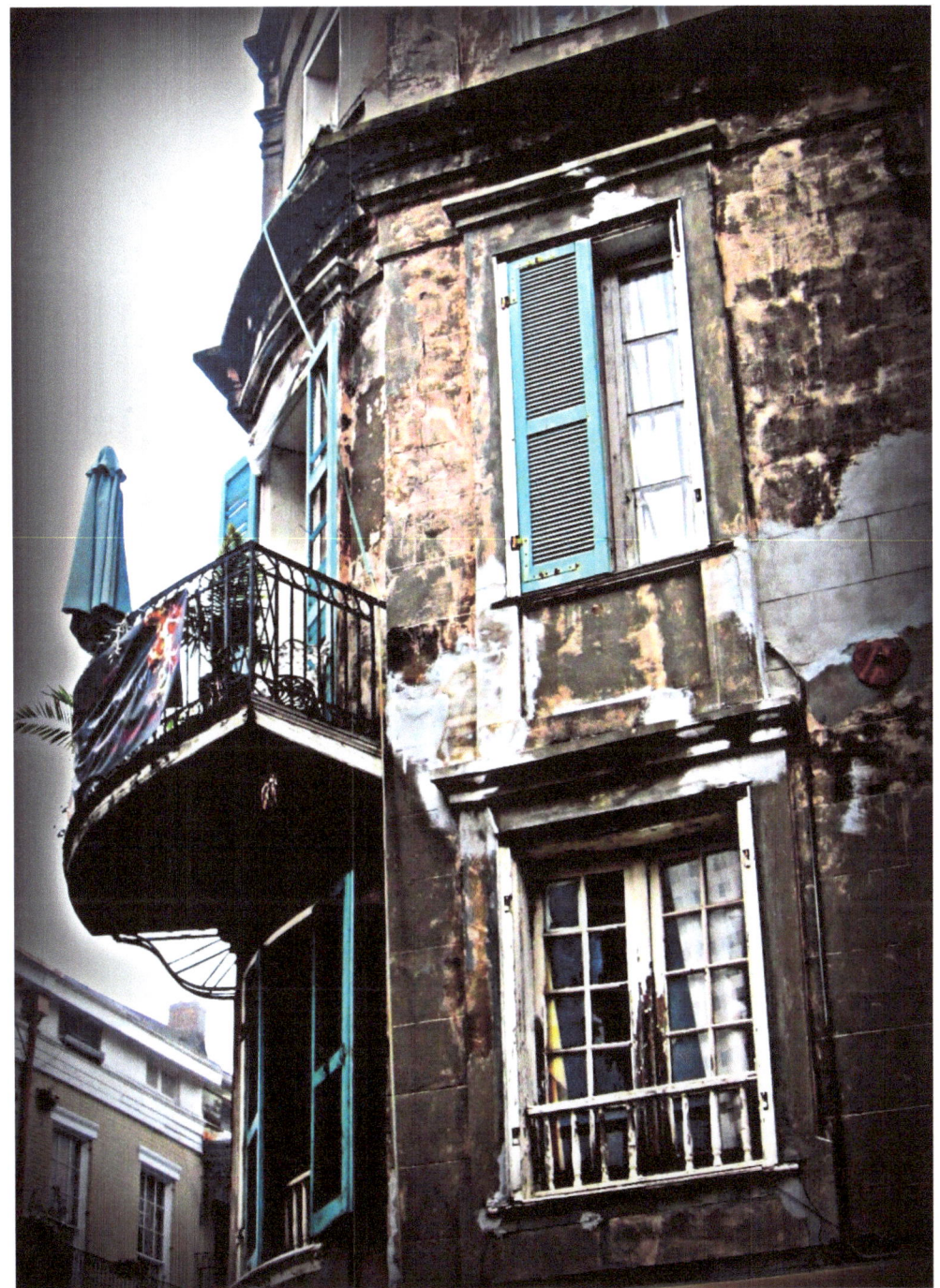

The Balcony Scene

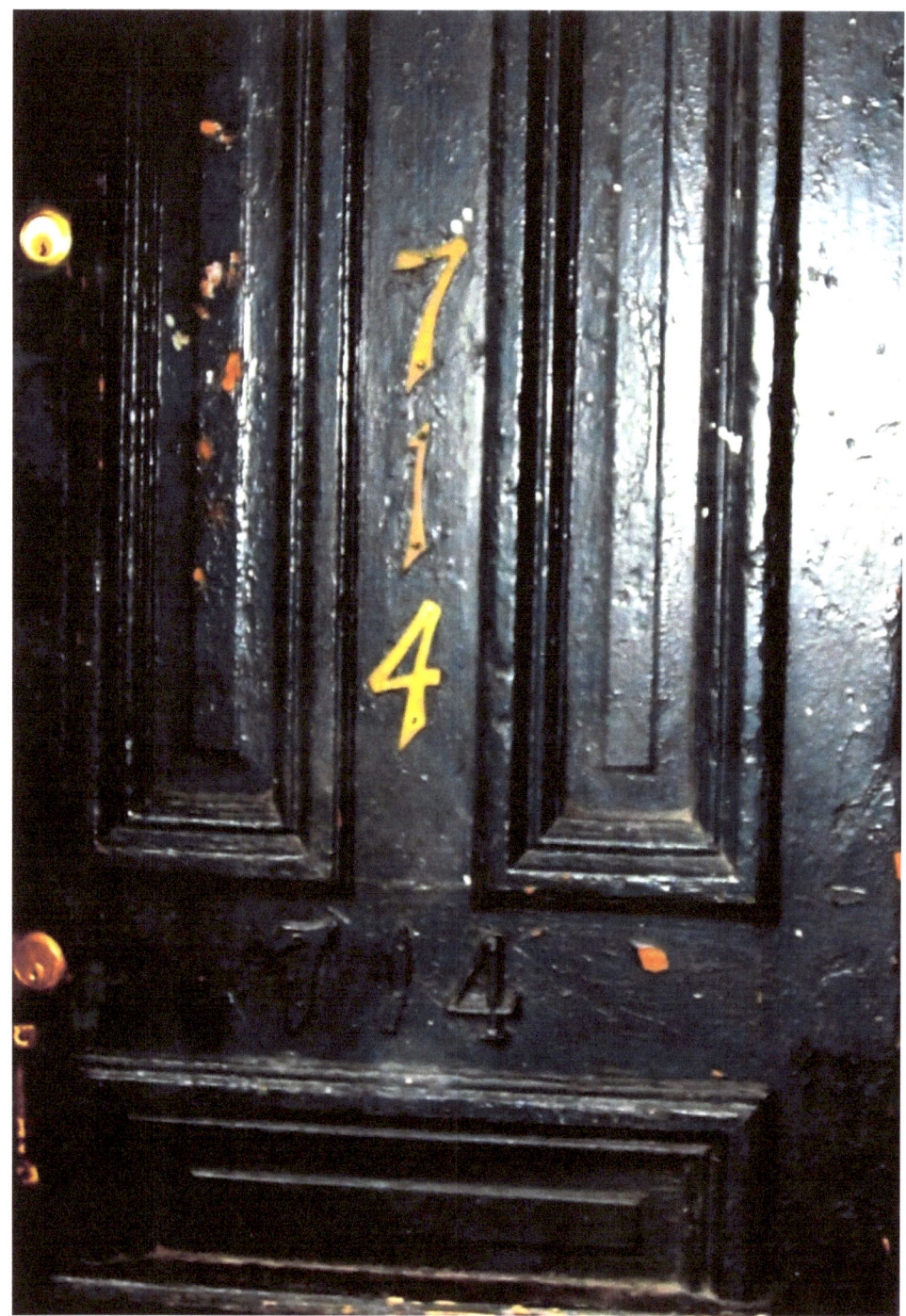

Number 714

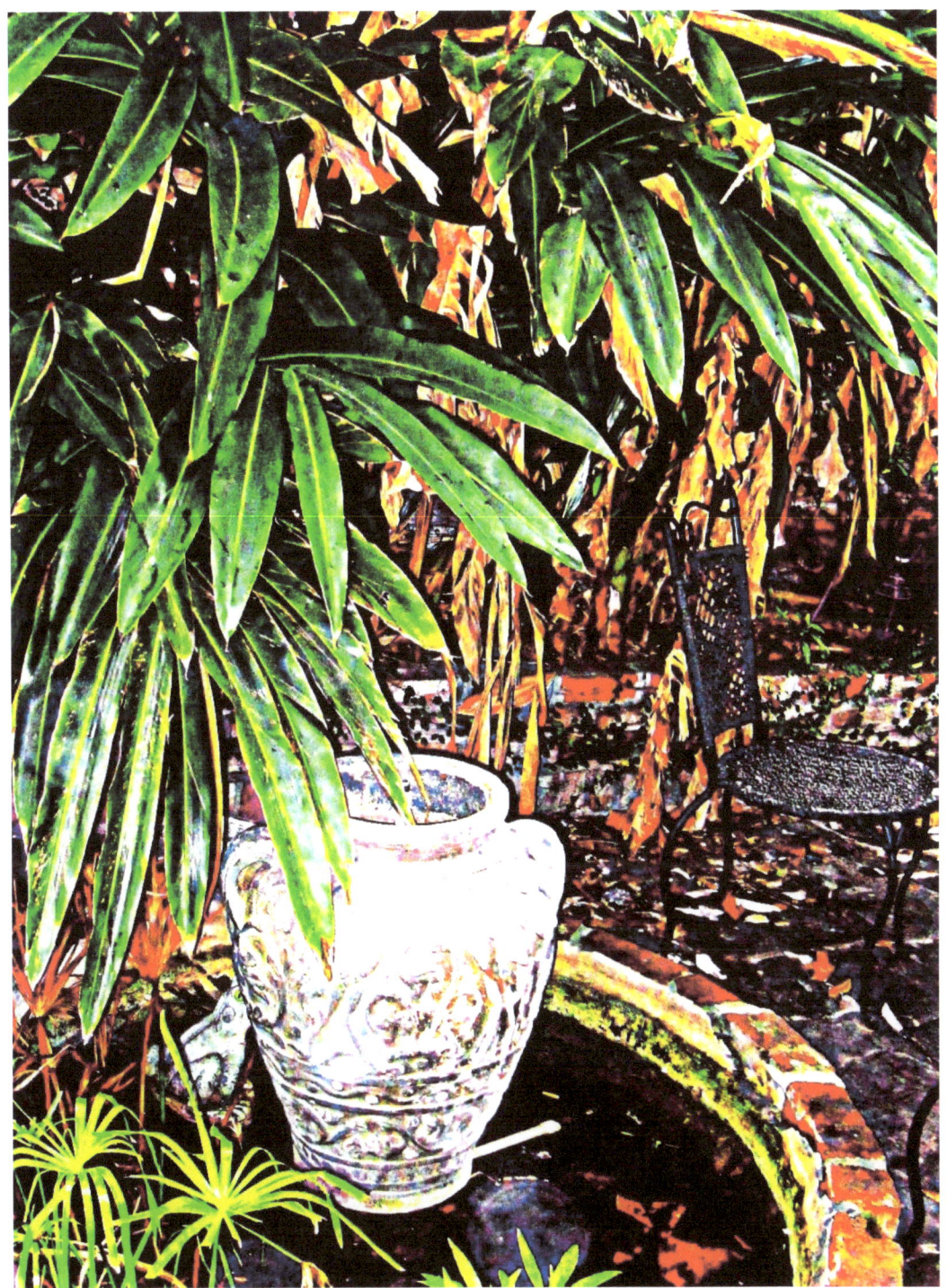

The Secret Garden

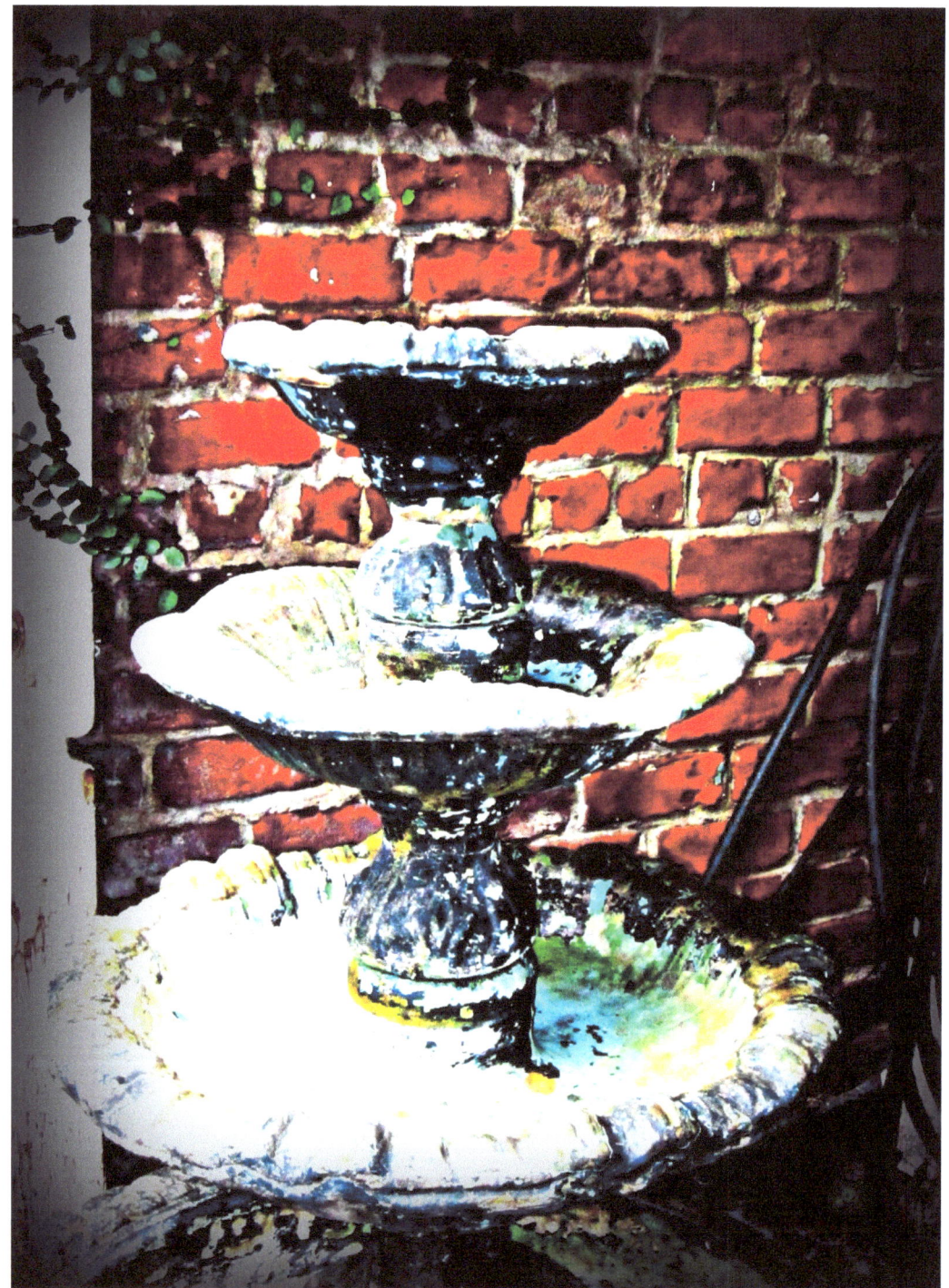

The Fountain of Youth

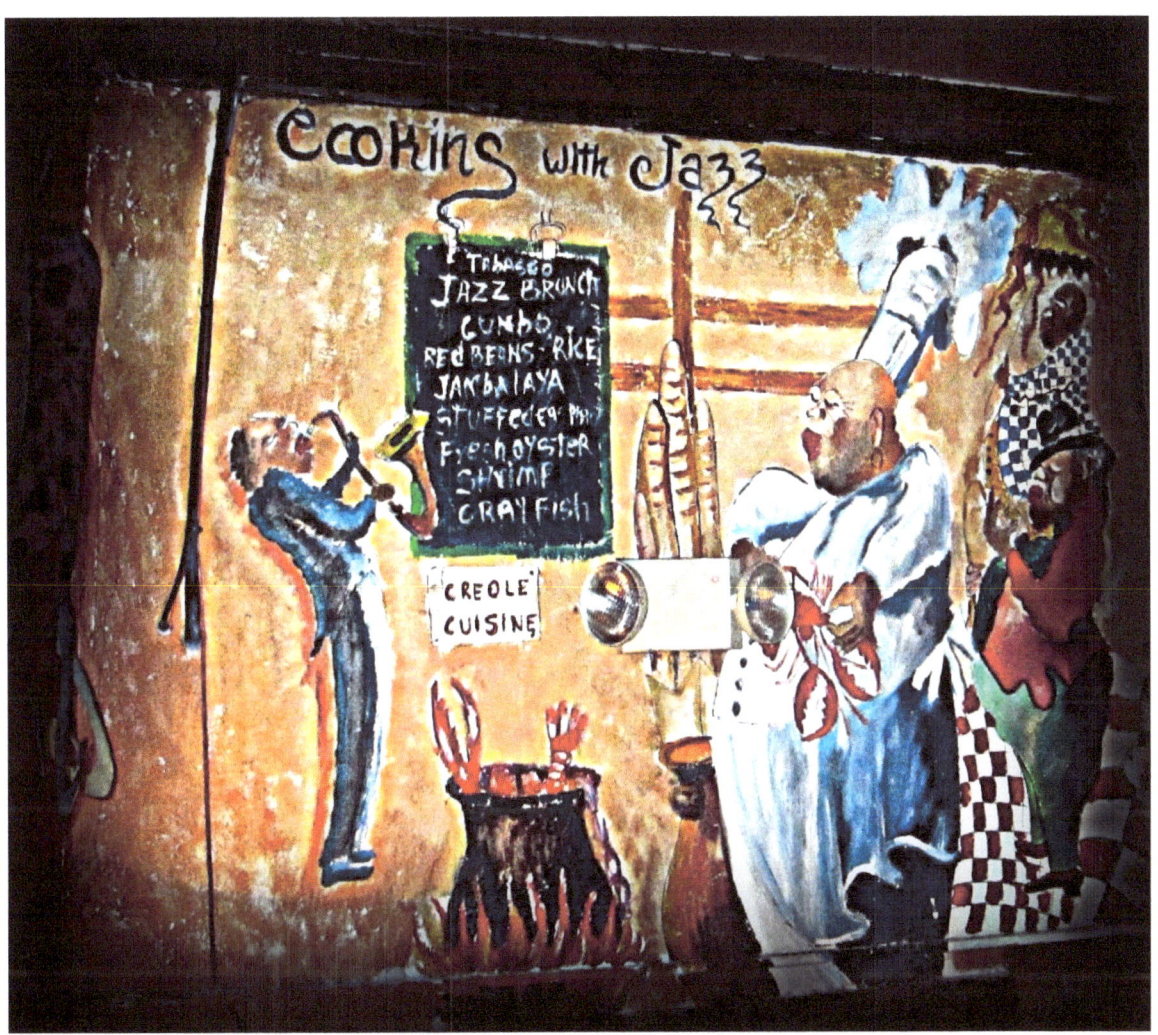

Cooking with Jazz in New Orleans

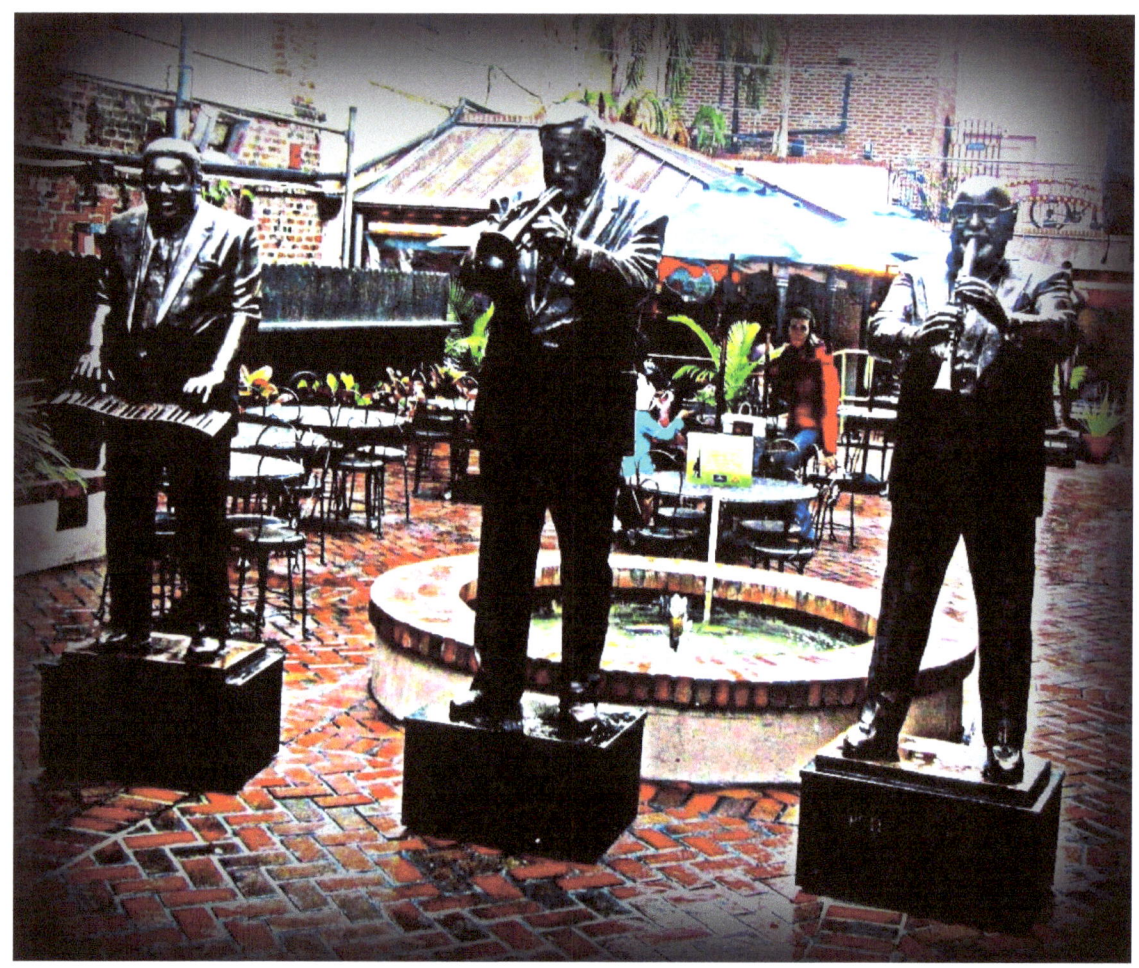

Bronze Jazz Trio
New Orleans

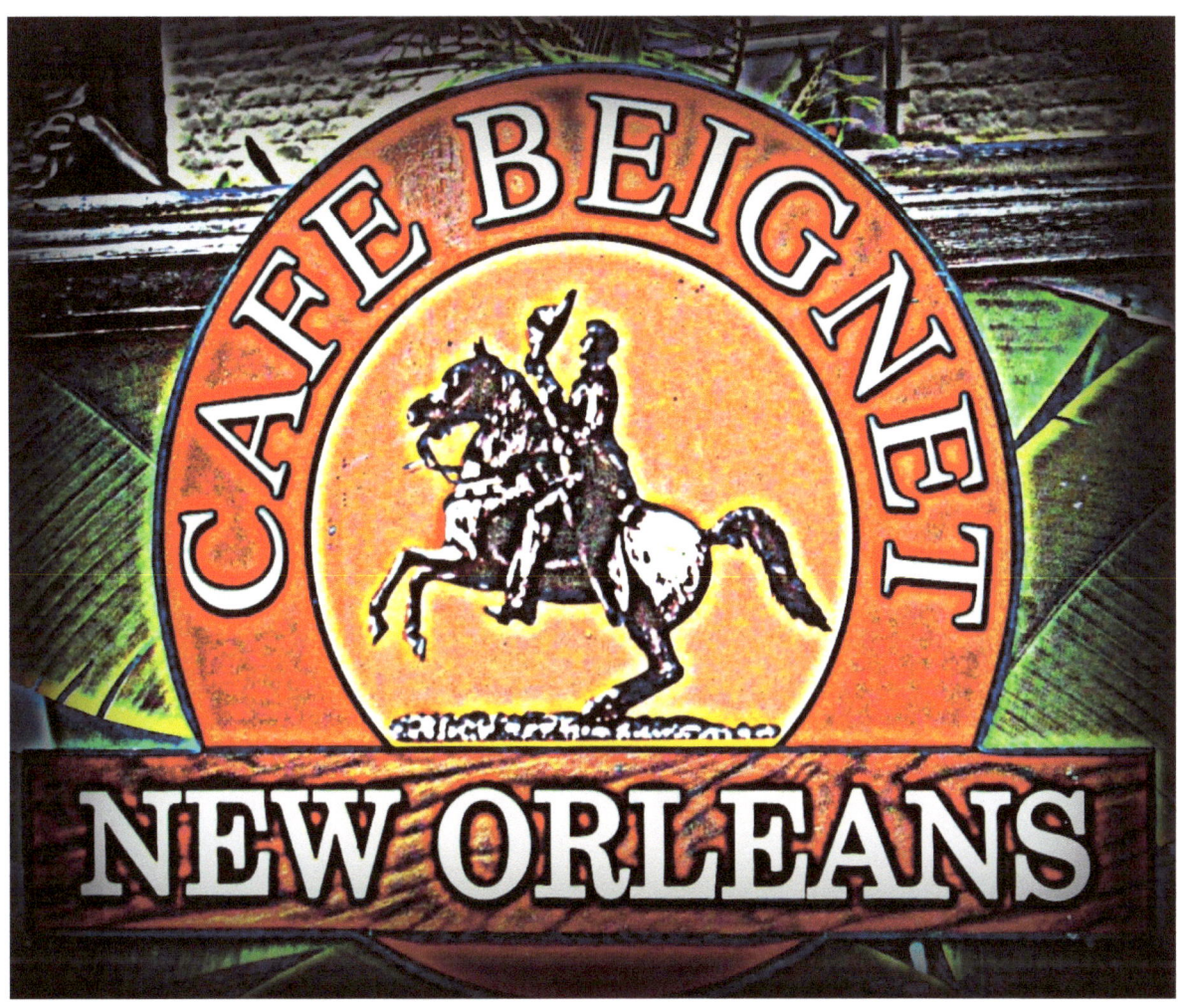

Late Night Snack

New Orleans

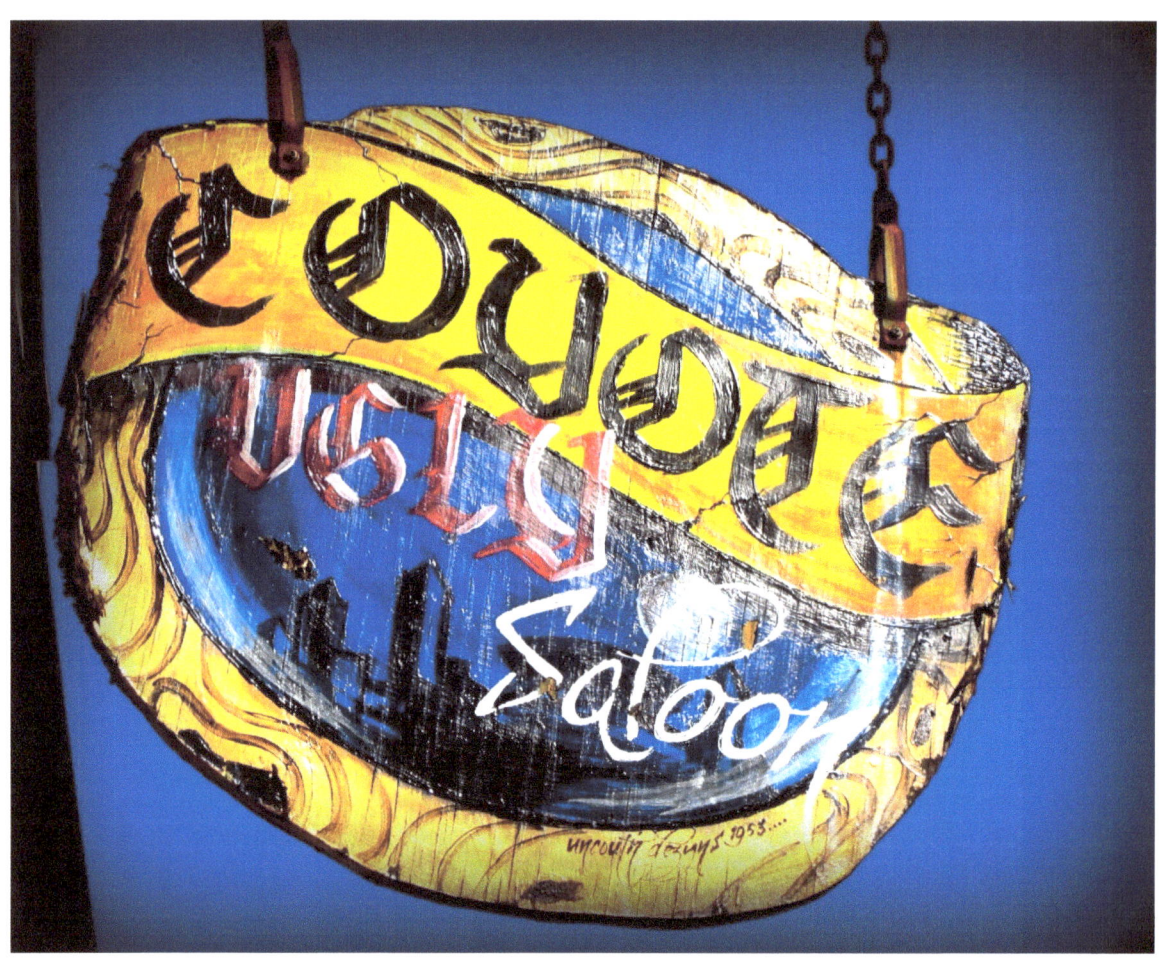

My Favorite Hangout

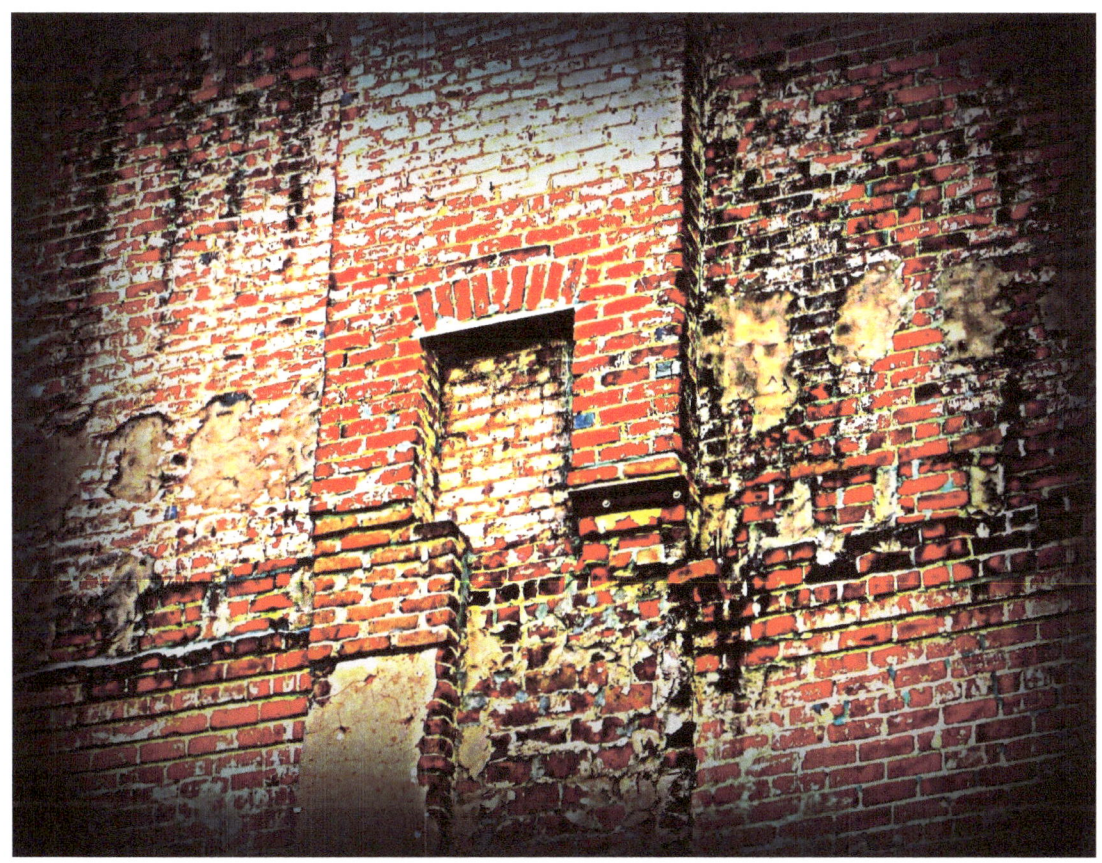

Back to the Wall

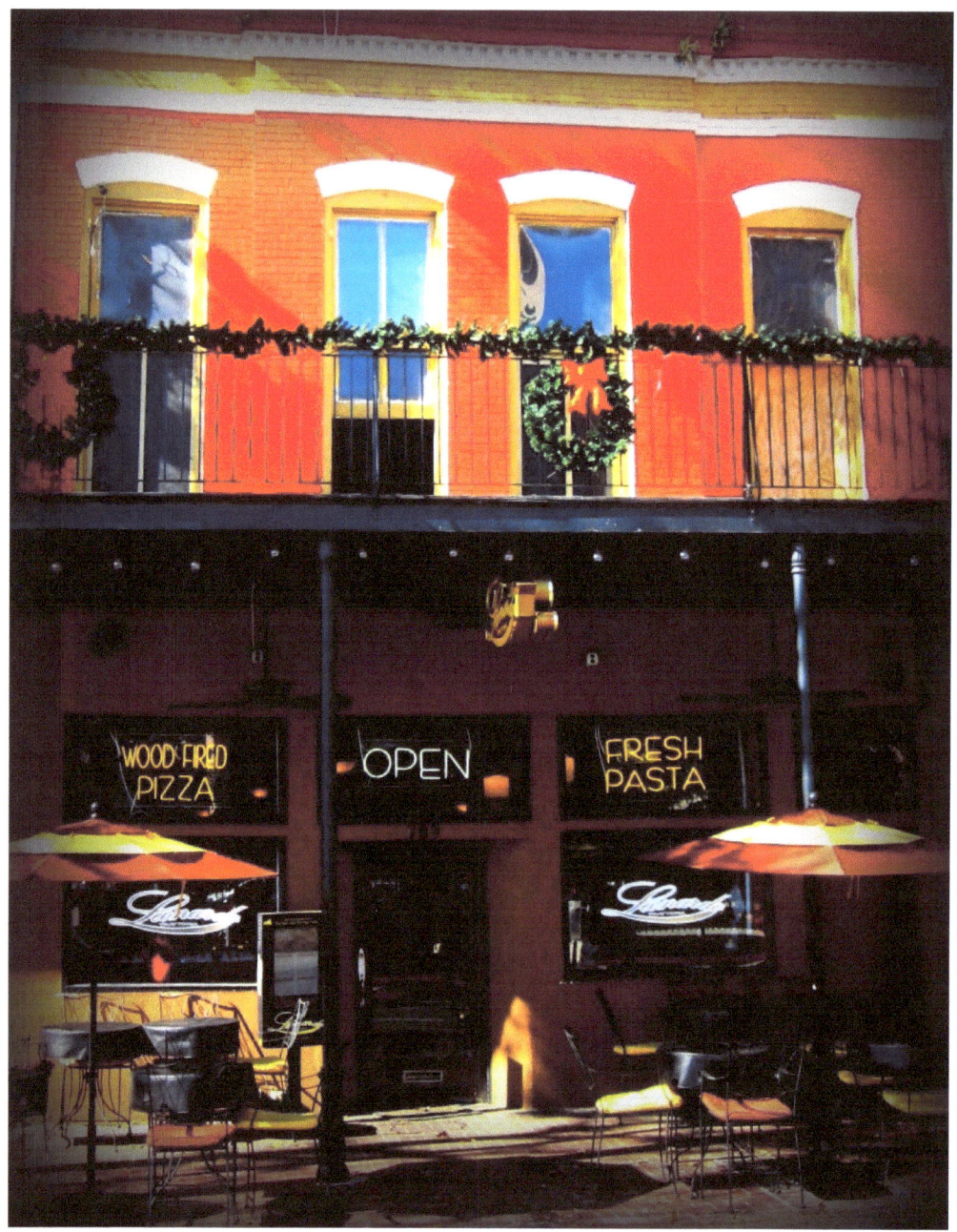

Time for a Moistener

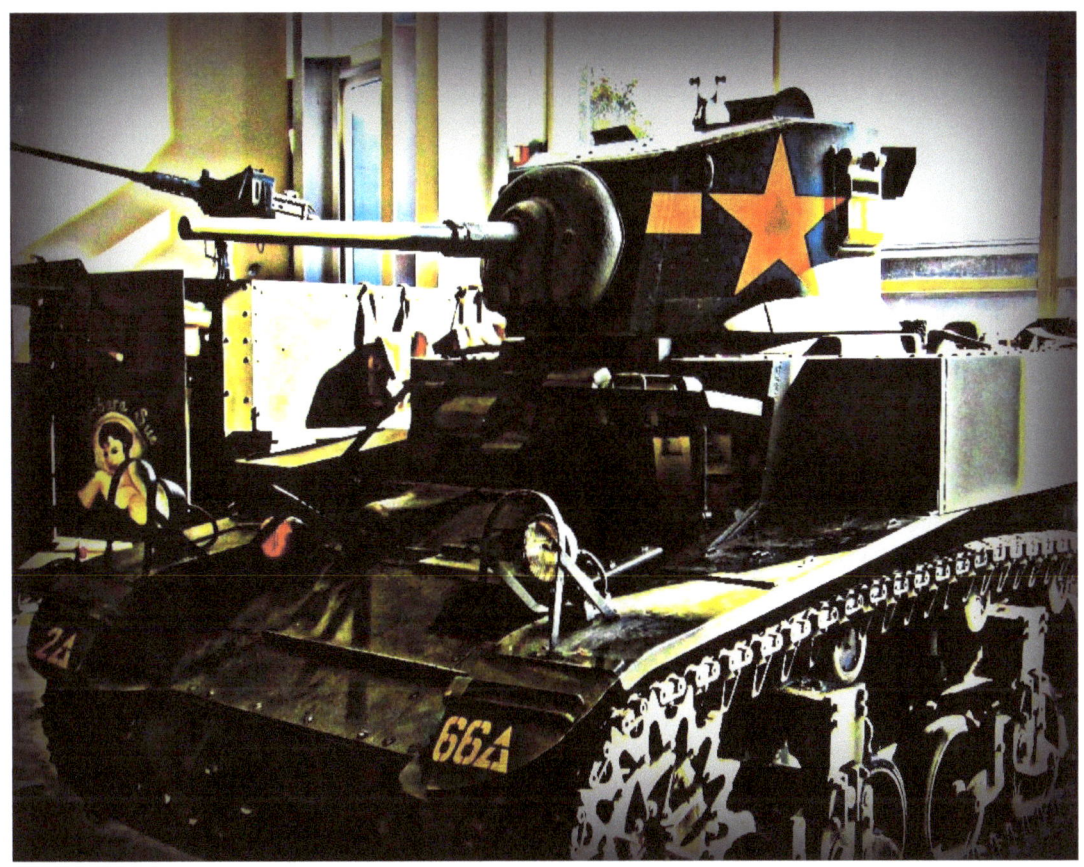

Tanks for the Memory

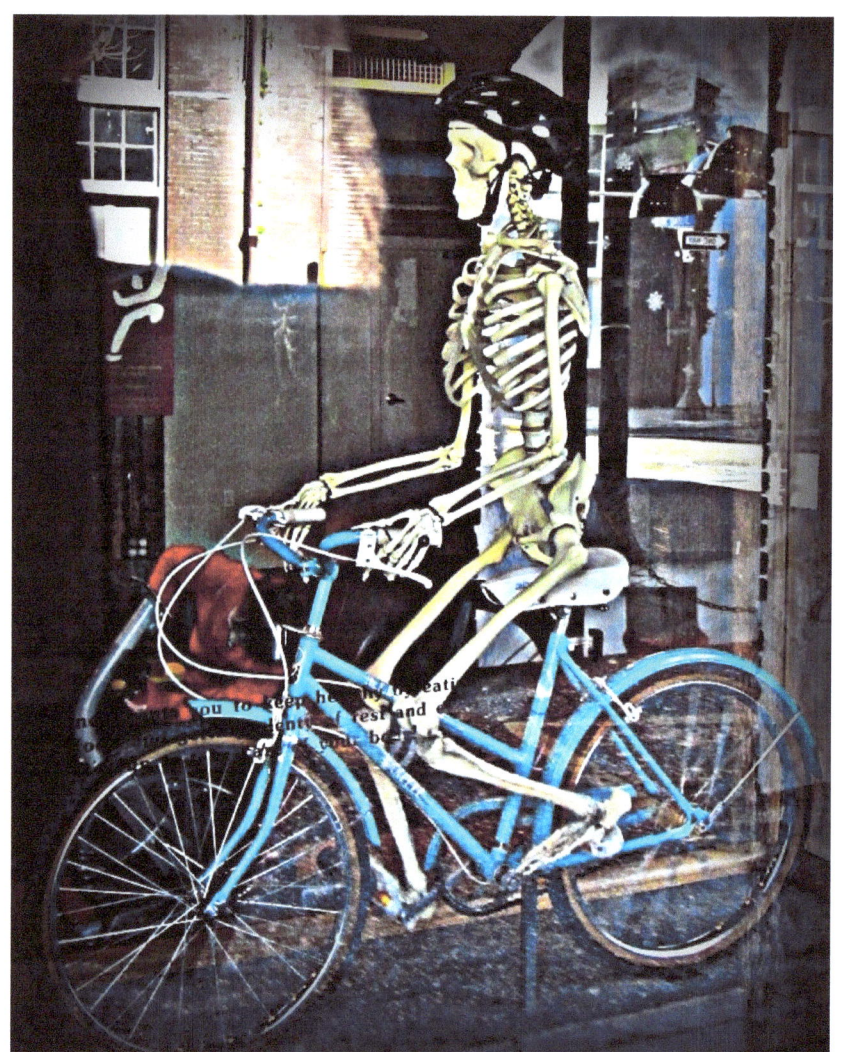

You Won't Catch Me Dead On A Bicycle

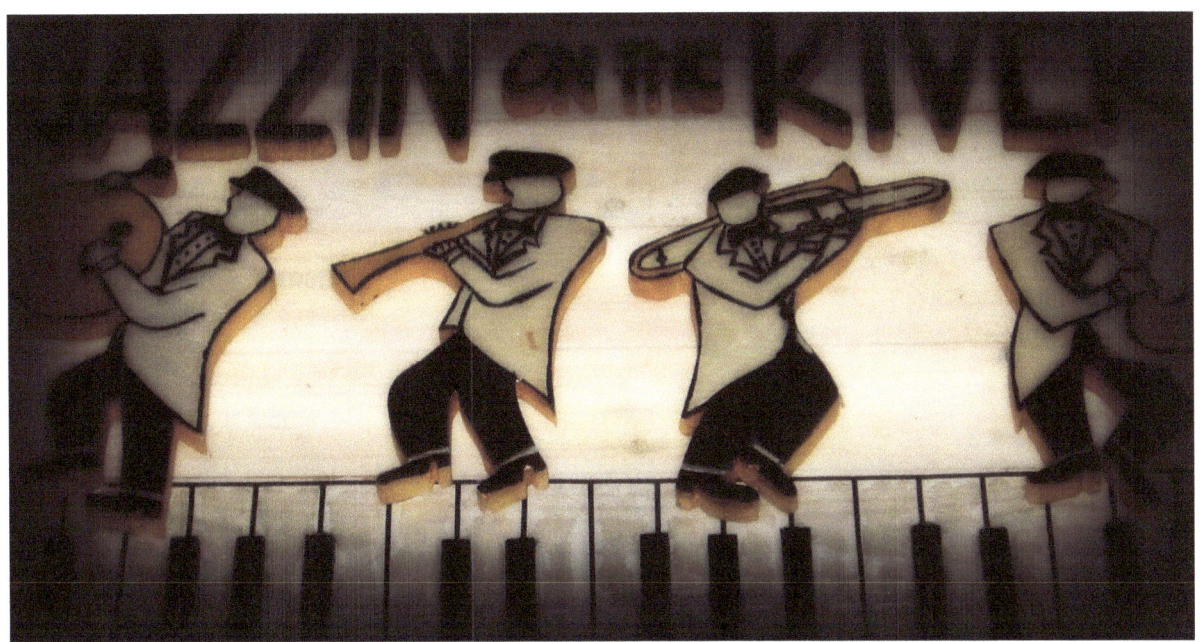

Jazz on the River

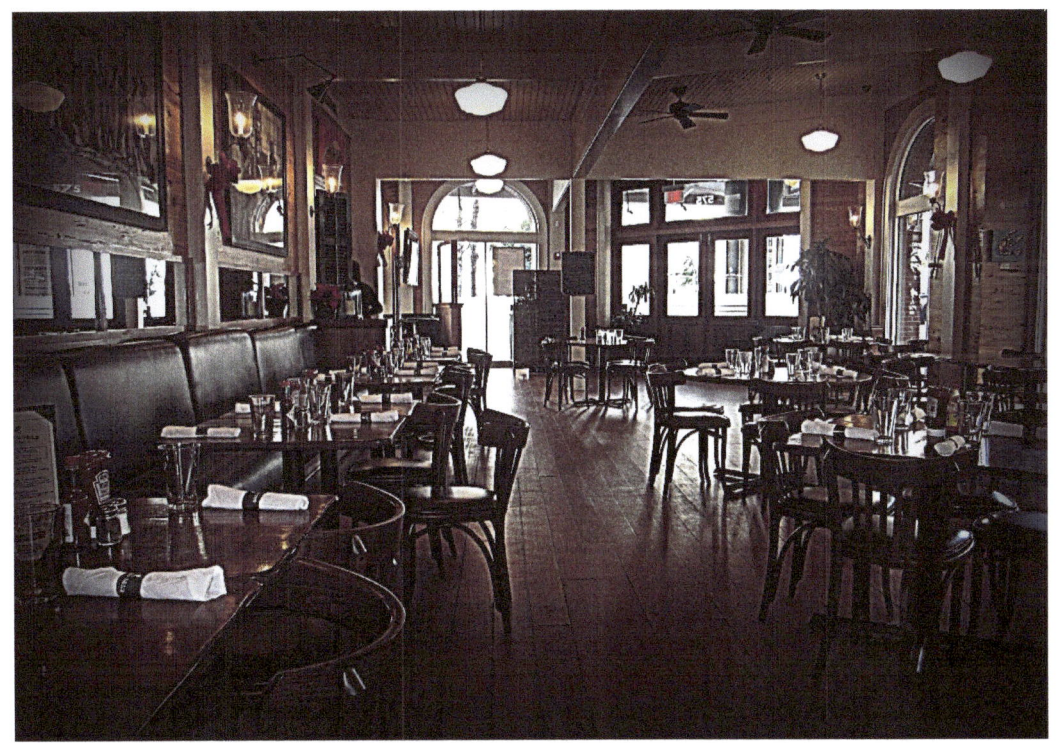

A Favorite Haunt in New Orleans

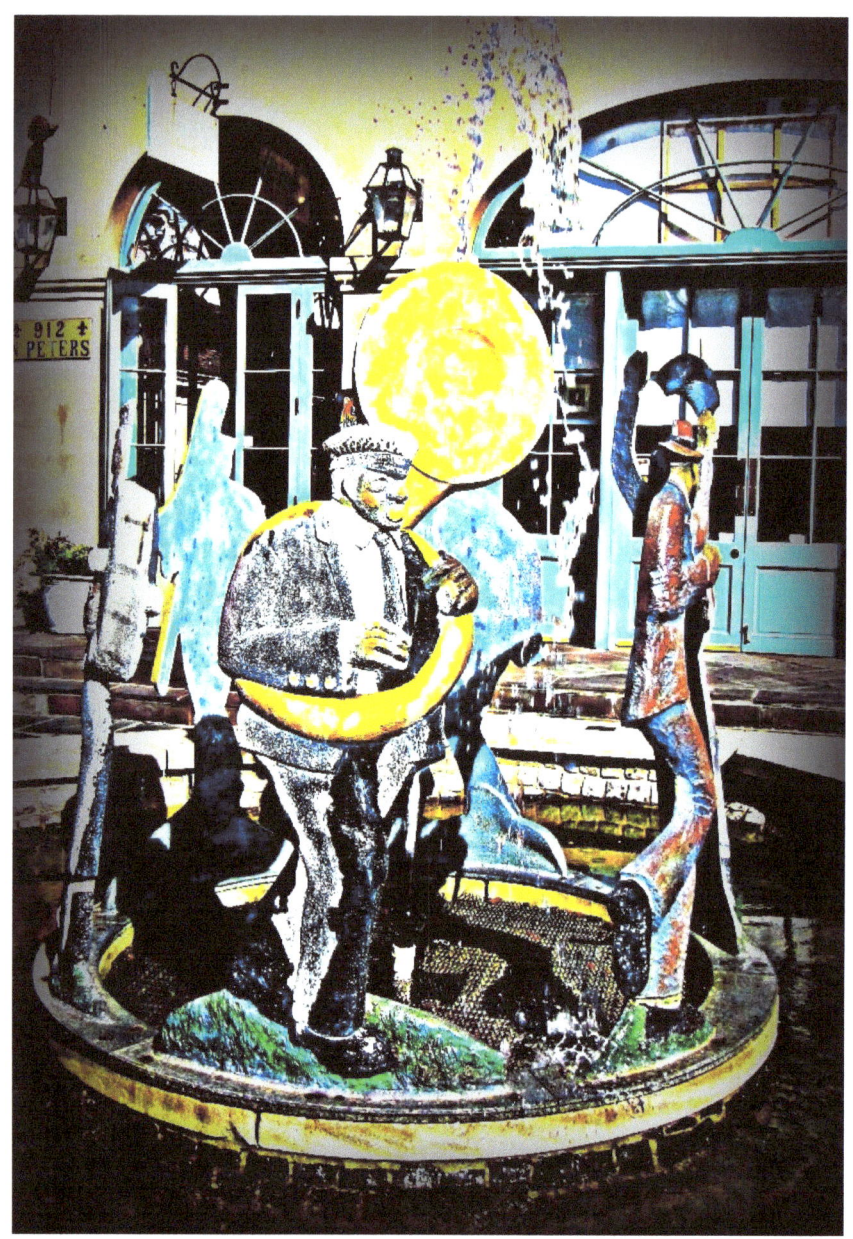

Heavy Metal Band

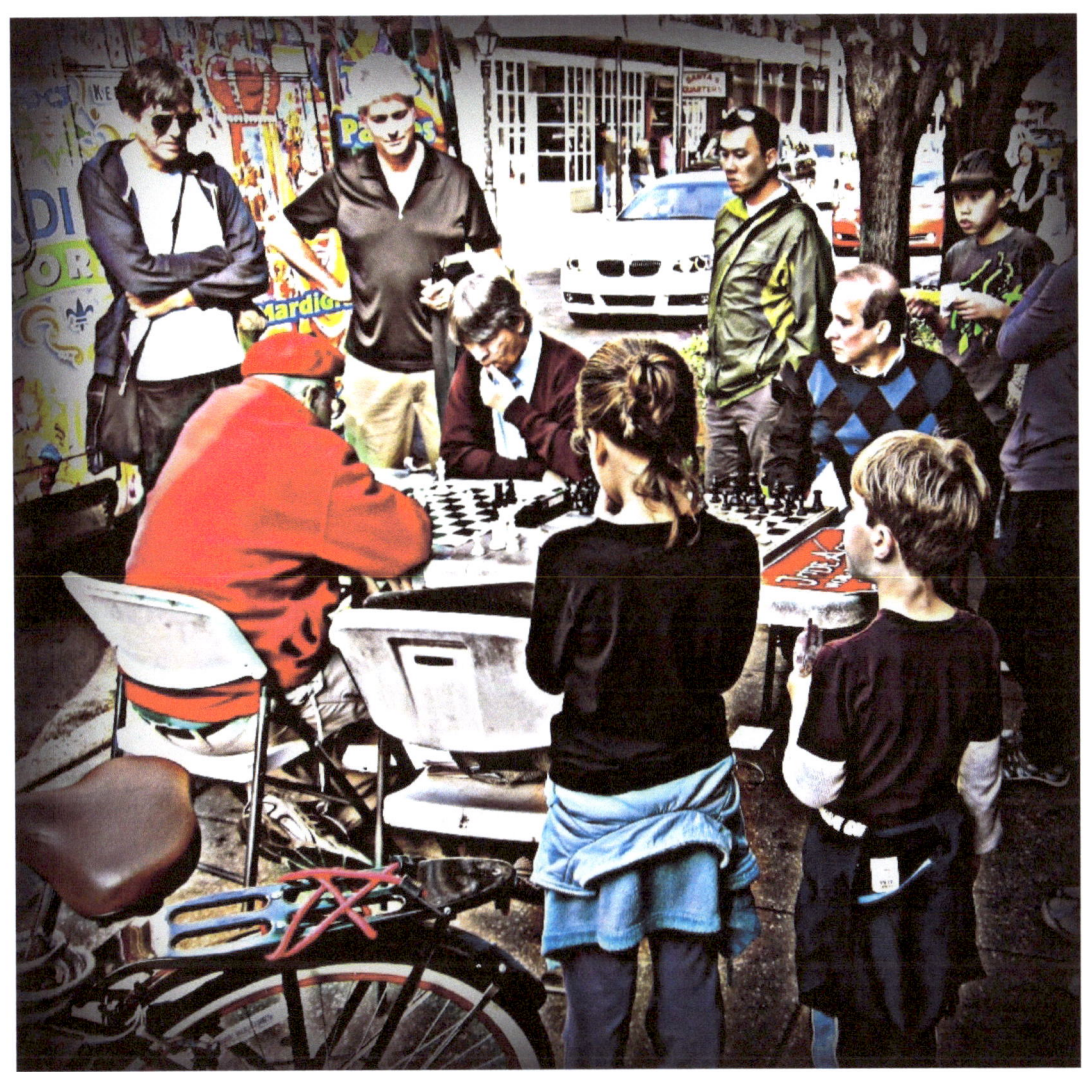

Got you!

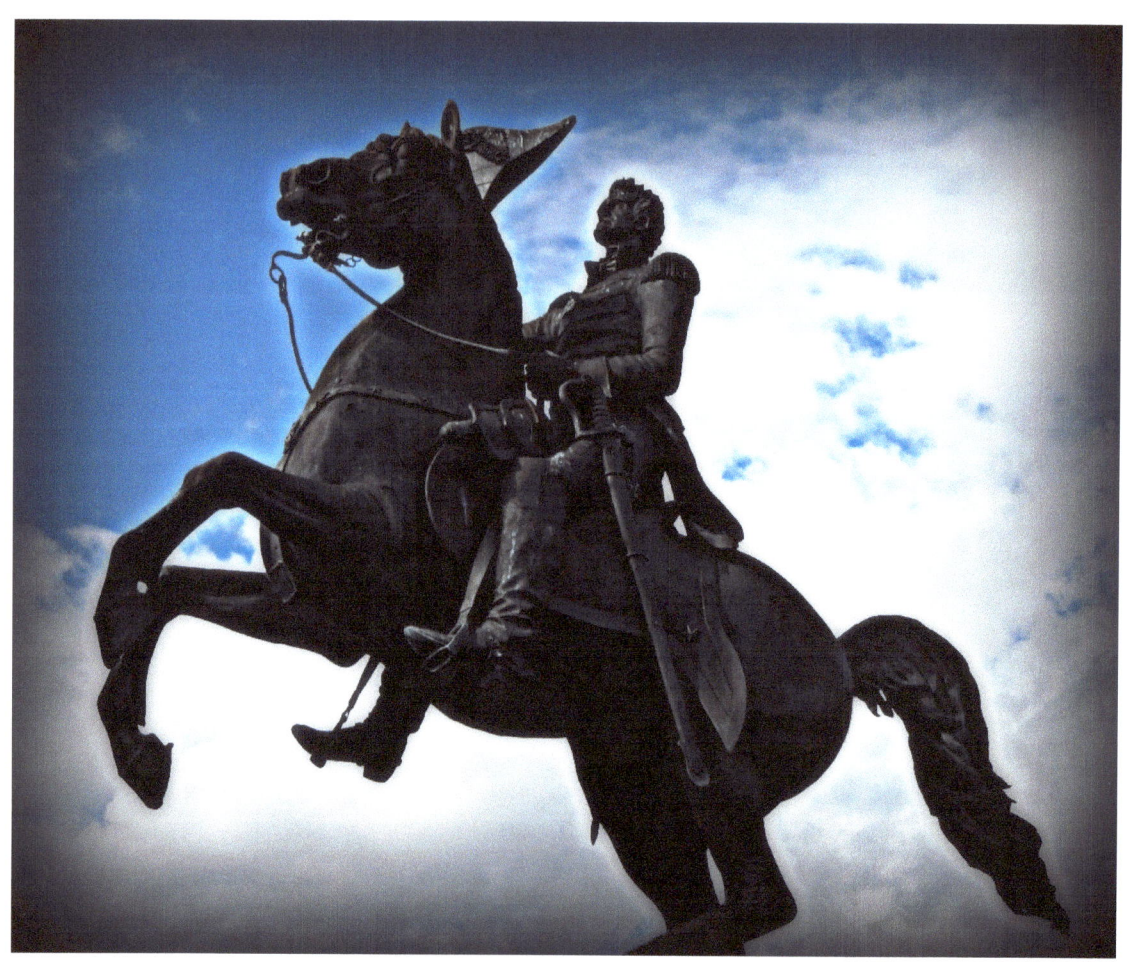

Rider of the Storm

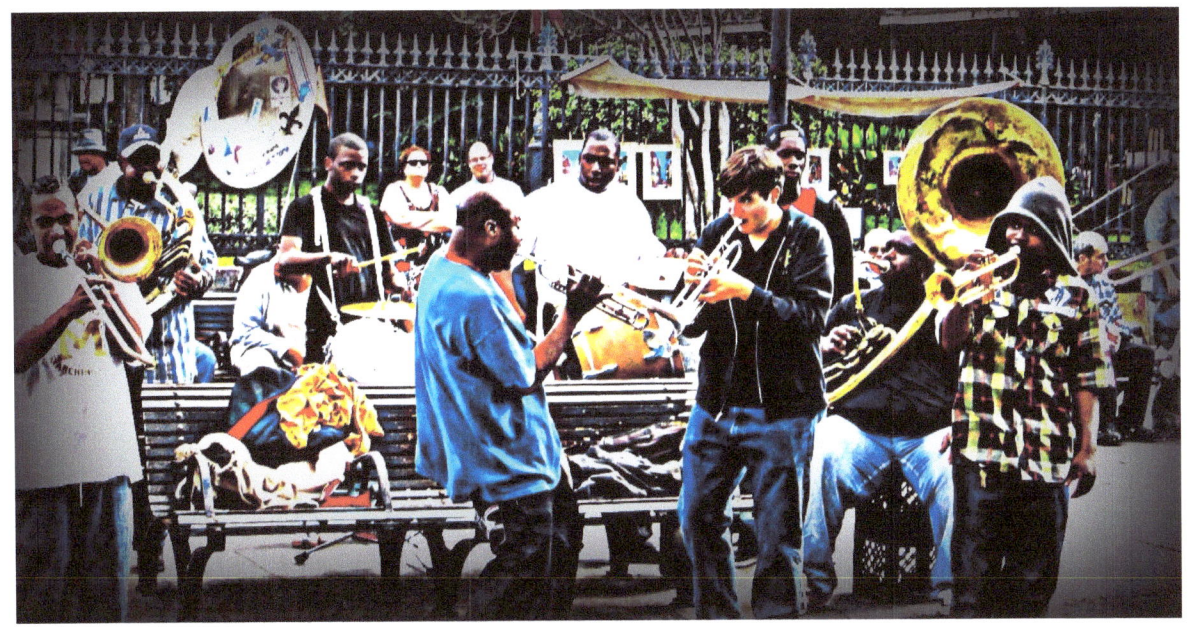

Jamming in New Orleans

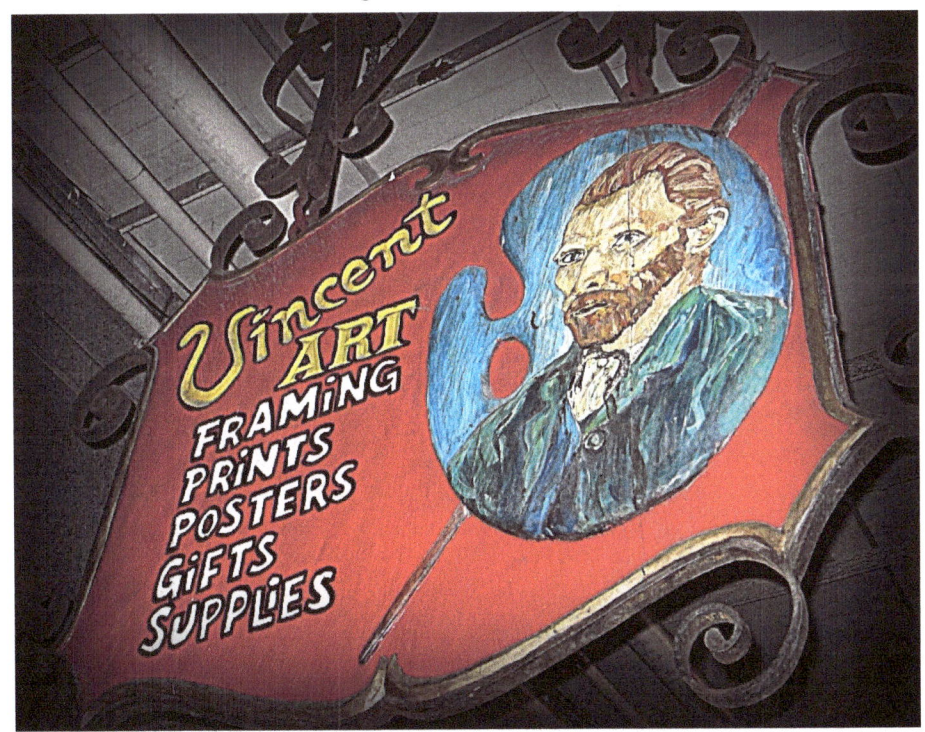

From Ear to Modernity

www.ingramcontent.com/pod-product-compliance
Lightning Source LLC
Chambersburg PA
CBHW051051180526
45172CB00002B/602